MAO ZEDONG, ZHOU ENLAI AND
OF THE CHINESE COMMUNIST LEADERSHIP

Nordic Institute Of Asian Studies
Recent and forthcoming studies on China

Børge Bakken (ed.): *Migration in China*

Vibeke Børdahl (ed.): *The Eternal Storyteller. Oral Literature in Modern China*

Kjeld Erik Brødsgaard and Mads Kirkebæk (eds): *China and Denmark. Relations since 1732*

Cecilia Milwertz: *Beijing Women Organizing for Change*

Donald B. Wagner: *The State and the Iron Industry in Han China*

David D. Wang: *Clouds over Tianshan. Essays on Social Disturbance in Xinjiang in the 1940s*

Jianping Wang: *Glossary of Chinese Islamic Terms*

Mao Zedong, Zhou Enlai and the Evolution of the Chinese Communist Leadership

Thomas Kampen

Mao Zedong, Zhou Enlai and the Evolution of the
Chinese Communist Leadership

First published in 2000 by NIAS Publishing
Reprinted in 2012 by NIAS Press
Nordic Institute of Asian Studies
Leifsgade 33, DK–2300 Copenhagen S, Denmark
tel: (+45) 3532 9501 • fax: (+45) 3532 9549
e–mail: books@nias.ku.dk
Web: http://www.niaspress.dk/

Typesetting by the Nordic Institute of Asian Studies
Printed and bound in Great Britain by
Marston Book Services Limited, Oxfordshire

British Library Cataloguing in Publication Data
Kampen, Thomas
Mao Zedong, Zhou Enlai and the evolution of the Chinese
communist leadership
1.Mao, Zedong, 1893-1976 2.Zhou, Enlai, 1898-1976
3.Zhong guo gong chan dang - History 4.China - Politics and
government - 1912-1949
I.Title - II.Nordic Institute of Asian Studies
324.2'51'075

ISBN 978-87-87062-80-0 (hardback)
ISBN 978-87-87062-76-3 (paperback)

Contents

Tables

Figures

Acknowledgements

I began my research on the history of the Chinese Communist Party and the career of Mao Zedong at the School of Oriental and African Studies (London) in the 1980s and continued in Beijing, Berlin, Heidelberg and Lund. This would not have been possible without the generous support of the British Council, the DAAD (Deutscher Akademischer Austauschdienst), the Friedrich-Ebert-Stiftung, the German Historical Institute (London) and the Centre for East and Southeast Asian Studies (Lund, Sweden).

Most of this book was written in 1996 and 1997 and revised in 1998. Thanks to all those at NIAS who helped me complete this work.

I would like also to thank Professors Tom Grunfeld, Marilyn Levine, Pamela Lubell, Michael Schoenhals, Stuart Schram, Patricia Stranahan, Natascha Vittinghoff, Erling von Mende and Rudolf Wagner for reading and commenting on the manuscript. Remaining problems are, of course, my responsibility.

Abbreviations

AM	Alternate Member
CC	Central Committee
CCP	Chinese Communist Party
CI	Communist International (Comintern)
ECCI	Executive Committee of the Comintern
KMT	Kuomintang [Guomindang]
M	Member
PB	Politburo
PRC	People's Republic of China

Author's Note

To avoid confusion, Chinese publications have been quoted with the author's full name, Western publications and Western translations of Chinese publications with the author's surname.

Chronology

July 1921	Founding of CCP (in Shanghai)
1924–1927	First KMT–CCP United Front
Autumn 1925	Establishment of Sun Yat-sen University (in Moscow)
June–July 1928	Sixth CCP Congress (in Moscow)
Spring 1930	Closure of Sun Yat-sen University
March 1930	Departure of Zhou Enlai (for Moscow)
August 1930	Return of Qu Qiubai and Zhou Enlai to Shanghai
September 1930	Third Plenum (in Shanghai)
December 1930	Arrival of Pavel Mif in Shanghai
January 1931	Fourth Plenum (in Shanghai)
January 1931	Establishment of Central Bureau (in Jiangxi)
April 1931	Arrival of Ren Bishi and Wang Jiaxiang in Jiangxi
June 1931	Arrest and execution of general secretary Xiang Zhongfa
September 1931	Establishment of provisional Party Centre led by Qin Bangxian
November 1931	First Soviet Congress (in Jiangxi)
December 1931	Arrival of Zhou Enlai in Jiangxi
October 1932	Ningdu Conference (in Jiangxi)
January 1933	Transfer of CCP Centre from Shanghai to Jiangxi
January 1934	Fifth Plenum (in Jiangxi)
October 1934	Beginning of Long March
January 1935	Zunyi Conference
February 1935	Zhang Wentian takes over Party leadership
July–August 1935	Seventh Comintern Congress (in Moscow)
December 1936	Xi'an Incident

1937–1945	Second KMT–CCP United Front (Anti-Japanese War)
November 1937	Arrival of Wang Ming, Kang Sheng and Chen Yun in Yan'an
Autumn 1938	Sixth Plenum (in Yan'an)
September 1941	Conference on CCP history, start of Rectification Movement
March 1943	Appointment of Mao Zedong (Politburo Chairman)
May 1943	Dissolution of Comintern
July 1943	Publication of first article praising *Mao Zedong Thought*
May 1944 – April 1945	Seventh Plenum (in Yan'an)
Summer 1944	First publication of the *Selected Works of Mao Zedong*
April–June 1945	Seventh CCP Congress (in Yan'an)
October 1949	Founding of the People's Republic of China
June 1951	Publication of Hu Qiaomu's *Thirty Years of the CPC*
1953	First publication of the *Resolution on Party History*

List of Key Protagonists

Chen Changhao (1906–67, from Hubei), joined Communist Party in 1930, studied in Moscow, participated in Long March, Central Committee member in 1930s and 1940s.

Chen Xiuliang (1907–98, from Zhejiang), joined Communist Party in 1926, studied in Moscow.

Chen Yu (1901–74, from Guangdong), joined Communist Party in 1925, studied in Moscow, Central Committee member from 1930s to 1970s.

Chen Yuandao (1901–33, from Anhui), joined Communist Party in 1925, studied in Moscow, executed in 1933.

Chen Yun (1905–95, from Jiangsu), joined Communist Party in 1925, participated in Long March, Politburo member from 1930s to 1980s.

Chiang Ching–kuo (1910–88, from Zhejiang), son and successor of KMT leader Chiang Kai–shek, studied in Moscow.

Chiang Kai–shek (1887–1975, from Zhejiang), KMT leader from 1920s to 1970s.

Deng Fa (1906–46, from Guangdong), joined Communist Party in 1925, member of Central Bureau in Jiangxi, Central Committee member in 1930s and 1940s, participated in Long March, died in an air crash.

Deng Xiaoping (1904–97, from Sichuan), joined Communist Party in 1924, studied in Moscow, participated in Long March, Politburo member from 1950s to 1980s.

Dong Biwu (1886–1975, from Hubei), joined Communist Party in 1921, participated in First CCP Congress, studied in Moscow, participated in Long March, Politburo member from 1940s to 1970s.

Gao Gang (1905–54, from Shaanxi), joined Communist Party in 1926, Politburo member in 1940s and 1950s.

Gu Zuolin (1908–34, from Jiangsu), joined Communist Party in 1926, member of Central Bureau in Jiangxi.

Guan Xiangying (1904–46, from Liaoning), joined Communist Party in 1925, studied in Moscow, participated in Long March.

He Kequan (1906–55, from Jiangxi), joined Communist Party in 1930, studied in Moscow, participated in Long March.

He Mengxiong (1898–1931, from Hunan), joined Communist Party in 1921, executed by KMT.

Hu Qiaomu (1912–92, from Jiangsu), joined Communist Party in 1932, secretary of Mao Zedong in 1940s, Central Committee member in 1950s and 1980s.

Kang Sheng (1898–1975, from Shandong), joined Communist Party in 1925, Politburo member from 1930s to 1970s.

Li Fuchun (1900–75, from Hunan), joined Communist Party in 1922, studied in Moscow, participated in Long March, Central Committee member from 1940s to 1970s.

Li Lisan (1899–1967, from Hunan), joined Communist Party in 1921, studied in France and Moscow, Central Committee member from 1920s to 1960s.

Li Weihan (1896–1984, from Hunan), joined Communist Party in 1922, participated in Long March, Central Committee member in 1920s and 1950s.

Lin Biao (1906–71, from Hubei), joined Communist Party in 1925, participated in Long March, Central Committee member from 1940s to 1970s.

Lin Boqu (1885–1960, from Hunan), joined Communist Party in 1921, participated in Long March, Central Committee member from 1930s to 1950s.

Lin Yunan (1898–1931, from Hubei), joined Communist Party in 1922, executed by KMT.

Lin Yuying (1897–1942, from Hubei), joined Communist Party in 1922, studied in Moscow.

Liu Shaoqi (1898–1969, from Hunan), joined Communist Party in 1921, studied in Moscow, participated in Long March, Politburo member from 1930s to 1960s.

Lu Futan (1890–1969, from Shandong), joined Communist Party in 1926, Politburo member in 1930s, arrested by KMT, executed by CCP.

Luo Dengxian (1905–33, from Guangdong), joined Communist Party in 1925, Politburo member in 1930s, arrested and executed by KMT.

Luo Ming (1900–87, from Guangdong), joined Communist Party in 1925, victim of campaign against 'Luo Ming line'.

Mao Zedong (1893–1976, from Hunan), joined Communist Party in 1921, participated in First CCP Congress, member of Central Bureau in Jiangxi, participated in Long March, CCP leader from 1943 to 1976.

Mao Zetan (1905–35, from Hunan), joined Communist Party in 1923, younger brother of Mao Zedong.

Nie Rongzhen (1899–1992, from Sichuan), joined Communist Party in 1923, military leader, participated in Long March, Central Committee member from 1940s to 1980s

Pan Hannian (1906–77, from Jiangsu), joined Communist Party in 1925, participated in Long March

Peng Dehuai (1898–1974, from Hunan), joined Communist Party in 1928, military leader, participated in Long March, Central Committee member from 1930s to 1950s.

Peng Zhen (1902–97, from Shanxi), joined Communist Party in 1923, Central Committee member in 1940s, 1950s, 1960s and 1980s.

Qin Bangxian (1907–46, from Zhejiang), joined Communist Party in 1925, studied in Moscow, participated in Long March, CCP leader from 1931 to 1935, Politburo member in 1930s and 1940s, died in an air crash.

Qu Qiubai (1899–1935, from Jiangsu), joined Communist Party in 1922, Politburo member in 1920s and 1930s, CCP leader in 1927 and 1928, executed by KMT.

Ren Bishi (1904–50, from Hunan), joined Communist Party in 1922, studied in Moscow, member of Central Bureau in Jiangxi, participated in Long March, Politburo member in 1930s and 1940s.

Shen Zemin (1902–33, from Zhejiang), joined Communist Party in 1921, studied in Moscow.

Wang Jiaxiang (1906–74, from Anhui), joined Communist Party in 1928, studied in Moscow, member of Central Bureau in Jiangxi, participated in Long March, Politburo member in 1930s and 1940s.

Wang Ming (1904–74, from Anhui), joined Communist Party in 1925, studied in Moscow, Politburo member in 1930s and 1940s, lived in Moscow from 1950s to 1970s.

Xia Xi (1901–36, from Hunan), joined Communist Party in 1921, studied in Moscow, Central Committee member in 1920s.

Xiang Ying (1898–1941, from Hubei), joined Communist Party in 1922, Politburo member from 1920s to 1940s, member of Central Bureau in Jiangxi, killed in South-Anhui Incident.

Xiang Zhongfa (1880–1931, from Hubei), joined Communist Party in 1922, CCP leader from 1928 to 1931, arrested and executed by KMT.

Yang Shangkun (1907–98, from Sichuan), joined Communist Party in 1926, studied in Moscow, participated in Long March, Central Committee member in 1950s and 1980s, PRC president from 1988 to 1993.

Ye Jianying (1897–1986, from Guangdong), joined Communist Party in 1927, military leader, participated in Long March, Central Committee member from 1940s to 1980s.

Zhang Guotao (1897–1979, from Jiangxi), joined Communist Party in 1921, participated in First CCP Congress, Politburo member in 1920s and 1930s, participated in Long March, defected to KMT in 1938.

Zhang Jinbao (1897–1984, from Anhui), joined Communist Party in 1926, Central Committee member in 1920s.

Zhang Qinqiu (1904–68, from Zhejiang), joined Communist Party in 1924, studied in Moscow, participated in Long March.

Zhang Wentian (1900–76, from Shanghai), joined Communist Party in 1925, studied in Moscow, CCP leader from 1935 to early 1940s.

Zhou Enlai (1898–1976, from Jiangsu), joined Communist Party in 1921, member of Central Bureau in Jiangxi, participated in Long March, Politburo member from 1920s to 1970s, prime minister from 1949 to 1976.

Zhu De (1886–1976, from Sichuan), joined Communist Party in 1922, military leader, studied in Germany and Moscow, member of Central Bureau in Jiangxi, participated in Long March, Politburo member from 1930s to 1970s.

Introduction

For about half a century, international research on the rise of Mao Zedong and the CCP leadership between 1931 and 1945 has been dominated by the idea of a 'two-line struggle'. According to this model, in 1935, Mao defeated the group of the '28 Bolsheviks' – which had taken over the leadership in 1931 – and led the CCP unchallenged until his death in 1976.

This model is simple and convinced many:

- For the fifteen years covered (and afterwards) only two major dates were important: January 1931 for the rise of the '28 Bolsheviks', and January 1935 for the fall of the '28 Bolsheviks' and the rise of Mao Zedong.

- There were only two major factions: on the one hand the '28 Bolsheviks' led by Wang Ming, and on the other Mao Zedong and his supporters. (Both groups could be identified with national interests: the '28 Bolsheviks' with Soviet interests, Mao with Chinese interests.)

I assume that there were several reasons why this simple model – which I shall only discuss in relation to CCP history between 1931 and 1945 – dominated international scholarship for such a long time. I do not intend to criticise particular scholars or publications but only highlight some general trends.

In the 1950s this model fitted well into the Cold War atmosphere (particularly with the use of the word 'Bolsheviks') when Western politicians (and scholars) observed and fought Soviet efforts to expand the 'communist bloc'.

When the Sino–Soviet conflict erupted in the 1960s the model confirmed 'long suspected' contradictions between China and the Soviet Union.

At the same time, the Soviet side also emphasised the decline of the CCP since Mao Zedong's takeover and the elimination of 'real Bolsheviks' during the Long March.

Following the escalation of the Vietnam War and the Soviet intervention in Prague in 1968, the anti-Soviet aspect of this model appealed to many Western scholars who identified Mao's rise with the liberation of Chinese communism from Stalinist control.

Origins of the model

However, many anti-communist and communist supporters of this model, which in the 1950s spread in the USA and other countries, did not realise that it was created in China and was formulated by the CCP leadership.

This model was based mainly on two Chinese publications of 1951 and 1953. (At this point earlier models of two-line struggles, like Wang Ming's model of 1930–31, will not be discussed.) In the spring of 1951, a year and a half after the founding of the People's Republic, preparations for the celebration of the thirtieth anniversary of the founding of the CCP began. Mao Zedong's secretary Hu Qiaomu was asked to produce a short survey of CCP history. Hu Qiaomu wrote and Mao Zedong revised *Thirty Years of the Communist Party of China*, which appeared in the *People's Daily* at the end of June. In the same year, the publication of the first official edition of the *Selected Works of Mao Tse-tung* started. The third volume, published in 1953, contained the (Central Committee) *Resolution on Some Questions in the History of Our Party*, which had been passed several years earlier, but had never been published. According to this document:

> The broad ranks of cadres and Party members who were opposed to the 'Left' line rallied around Comrade Mao Tse-tung as their leader; and this made it possible for the enlarged meeting of the Central Political Bureau, convened at Tsunyi, Kweichow [Zunyi, Guizhou], in January 1935 under the leadership of Comrade Mao Tse-tung, to succeed in terminating the rule of the 'Left' line in the Central Committee and in saving the Party

2

at a most critical juncture. [...] The meeting inaugurated a new leadership in the Central Committee with Comrade Mao Tse-tung at the head, and this was a change of paramount historical importance in the Chinese Party. (Central Committee 1953: 188)

In these texts the importance of the Zunyi Conference (January 1935) for the Party, Army and Mao Zedong's rise was, for the first time, officially and publicly proclaimed.

Since 1951, this interpretation was always upheld and it was repeated in the 1981 *Resolution on Certain Questions in the History of Our Party since the Founding of the People's Republic of China.*

Chinese historiography

In the People's Republic of China the simplicity and some implications of this model established in the early 1950s were also welcomed. For – old and new – supporters of Mao the postulated clear and early victory and the unchallenged leadership of Mao since 1935 was reassuring. For his enemies the decision to mention only two names of 'negative' persons explicitly – Wang Ming and Qin Bangxian – probably brought some comfort. For several reasons, particularly because of the close relations with the Soviet Union, the term '28 Bolsheviks' was not used in China; instead other phrases like 'Wang Ming's and Qin Bangxian's "left" deviation (line)' were used and the roles of Stalin and the Comintern were not mentioned; only overseas Chinese, Taiwanese and Western scholars used the term '28 Bolsheviks'. Even after the Sino–Soviet conflict erupted, the old terminology continued to be used, as the Chinese leadership argued that the conflict with Khrushchev and Brezhnev was caused by their deviation from the correct line of Stalin; therefore the role of Stalin and the Comintern could not be criticised.

Only in unofficial texts of the Cultural Revolution – particularly in Red Guard publications – were the Soviet Union and their 'supporters' in China heavily criticised and Mao's 'victory' over the '28 Bolsheviks' during the Long March was praised. After the end of the Cultural Revolution this irregular situation was ended and the term '28 Bolsheviks' no longer used; the above-mentioned *Resolution* of 1981 reinstated the traditional interpretation of CCP history.

At that time, Chen Yun, Deng Xiaoping and Yang Shangkun, who had participated in the Long March, were rehabilitated and elected to the Politburo. It was not surprising that their long revolutionary careers were praised and this included their participation in the Long March and the Zunyi Conference. As the fiftieth anniversary of the conference was approaching, the date for suitable publications was obvious. The problem was, however, that the surviving participants of the Zunyi Conference had belonged either to the losing side or did not play an important role. Thus, it was also necessary to propagate the 'success' and 'importance' of the Zunyi Conference without providing too many details: the 'historical' event could only be praised as long as no unnecessary information was leaked. The activities in 1985 and the publication of the *Documents of the Zunyi Conference* in the same year, were, in that respect, quite successful.

Western scholarship

For Western scholars in the 1950s, there was hardly a problem of dates and facts contradicting intended interpretations, as the Chinese publications only presented a model, but no sources, and because there were not enough reliable sources in the West.

Among the materials on CCP history available in the 1950s and 1960s there were a number of CCP documents and communist publications captured by the KMT. These were often anonymous or signed with unidentifiable pseudonyms and included plans, aims and intentions, which were often not realised. There were also some autobiographical accounts by former communists. But due to the bitterness of the authors, who had often been involved in lengthy factional struggles or served long prison terms, these accounts were very subjective and they could not be verified. As most arrests were made in Shanghai in the late 1920s and early 1930s, the reports of prisoners did not cover the Jiangxi Soviet, the Long March and Yan'an.

At that time the lack of the following four types of sources was obvious:

- Biographical sources, providing information on birth dates and places, social background and education, as well as CCP entry and political activities.
- Sources on the structure of the Communist Party, its Central Committee, Politburo, Secretariat, departments and commissions.

- Detailed chronological data on important events in CCP history, including Party congresses, plenary sessions and conferences.

- Authentic, complete and correctly dated CCP documents by identifiable author(s).

Since the 1950s, this lack of sources was particularly evident when 'factional struggles' in the PRC were studied. The earliest major internal struggles already contradicted the 'two-line model' as the first victims were Gao Gang (1954) and Peng Dehuai (1959), who had both been regarded as supporters of Mao Zedong. The cases of Liu Shaoqi (1966) and Lin Biao (1971), were even worse because both had been leading politicians on Mao's side and opponents of the '28 Bolsheviks'. At the same time the political survival of Zhou Enlai was remarkable and confusing, as it was known or, at least, assumed, that he had closely co-operated with the '28 Bolsheviks' in the 1930s.

These problems inspired and encouraged Western research, but due to the lack of reliable sources in the 1950s, 1960s and 1970s they could not be solved.

New sources

In connection with the rehabilitation of politicians purged before and during the Cultural Revolution, the re-evaluation of the roles of Mao Zedong and Liu Shaoqi and the preparation of the trial of the 'Gang of Four', a reappraisal of CCP history started in the People's Republic of China at the end of the 1970s. This led to an unprecedented expansion of research and a flood of publications in the 1980s. (In connection with the above-mentioned cases – Gao Gang, Peng Dehuai, Liu Shaoqi and, particularly, Lin Biao – there had also been intensive internal discussions and investigations concerning numerous persons and events in CCP history, but, with the exception of the early phase of the Cultural Revolution, both the discussions and the results were kept secret.)

The most important sources for the present book are publications from the People's Republic published since the early 1980s, including:

- Memoirs, autobiographies and biographies
- Collections of CCP documents
- Descriptions of the organisational structure of the CCP
- Chronicles of the Party and several politicians
- Books and articles by historians

Contents

It is obvious that the above-mentioned two-line model is not suitable for the analysis of political developments after 1949. In this book the suitability of the model for studying the period before 1949 will be tested. The following questions will be asked:

- Did Mao become CCP leader in 1935 or at another time?
- Who supported Mao and made his rise possible?
- Who lost the power struggle?
- Did Mao rise with the support of the Communist International or against its wishes, and would that indicate that the Comintern lost control and the CCP gained independence?

The Zunyi Conference of 1935 is a central problem because this was the time when, according to the two-line model, the rule of the '28 Bolsheviks' ended and Mao's takeover happened. Before the 'winner' is discussed, it should first be asked if the 'losers' really ruled the CCP from 1931 to 1935. Therefore this study will start with the alleged 'takeover' of the '28 Bolsheviks' in winter 1930–31. The book ends with the Seventh CCP Congress in 1945, when Mao Zedong was elected chairman of the Central Committee.

As most of the early Western accounts of CCP history were written without detailed knowledge of the biographies of the '28 Bolsheviks', the identification of the people involved and the analysis of their background are important elements of this study. Since the statements about the '28 Bolsheviks' are characterised by general assumptions on their homogeneity, relating to background, age, education and political experience, simple data concerning the years and places of birth, family background, Party entry and studies abroad can be used to verify or reject established interpretations. This has the advantage that simple data without political significance can be used to get important results. This method also reduces the dependence on accounts which are influenced by political or moral assessments.

On the basis of these Chinese publications of the years 1979–95, the rise of Mao Zedong and important changes in the Party leadership between 1931 and 1945 will be analysed. The results are compared with Western accounts of CCP history; these are mainly publications by American, English, German and French scholars published between 1949 and 1995.

The emphasis lies mainly on the detailed analysis of the composition of the leading bodies of the CCP (Central Committee, Politburo and Secretariat) and the clarification of the formal positions of leading Party members at different times. The identification of exact dates of major political and military events is of great importance. Thus it will also be possible to provide dates for the return and 'takeover' of the '28 Bolsheviks' as well as the rise of Mao Zedong.

The comparison of Western accounts with recent Chinese publications questions many assumptions concerning CCP history. Particularly the history of the rise of the '28 Bolsheviks' and their confrontation with Mao Zedong is more complicated than described before. The detailed study of recent Chinese sources also lead to doubts concerning the rise of Mao Zedong in 1935 and concerning the independence of the CCP from the Comintern after 1935.

These problems will be examined in the following way:

At the beginning the identity and origins of the '28 Bolsheviks' will be analysed and the situation of the CCP in 1930 will be described (Chapter 1).

Then the 'takeover' of the Party centre in Shanghai by the '28 Bolsheviks' in 1931 and the role of the Comintern in Li Lisan's downfall will be discussed (Chapter 2).

This is followed by an analysis of the 'confrontation' between the '28 Bolsheviks' and Mao Zedong in the Jiangxi Soviet (Chapter 3).

In the following chapter (Chapter 4), the 'takeover' by Mao Zedong during the Long March (1934–35) and the role of several other Party leaders will be studied.

After that, the complicated relations between the CCP and Comintern after the Long March and the establishment of the Second United Front will be described (Chapter 5).

Finally, Mao Zedong's rise to chairman of the Politburo in the first half of the 1940s will be analysed (Chapter 6).

Figure 1: Mao Zedong (*right*) with his mother and his brothers Mao Zemin and Mao Zetan (1919).

ONE

The Leadership of the Chinese Communist Party and the Return of the '28 Bolsheviks' (1930)

The return of the '28 Bolsheviks' from Moscow in 1930 and their confrontation with Li Lisan has long been regarded as the first step in their takeover of the CCP leadership. Before describing this process, the state of the leadership in 1930 will be discussed briefly; then the identity and background of the '28 Bolsheviks' and the confrontation with Li Lisan will be described.

THE LEADERSHIP OF THE CCP IN 1930

In the *Cambridge History of China*, Jerome Ch'en provided the following list of CCP leaders for the years after the end of the First United Front in summer 1927:

> Ch'en Tu-hsiu's [Chen Duxiu's] leadership of the CCP had ended in mid-1927. His successors were younger men – Ch'ü Ch'iu-pai [Qu Qiubai] in the second half of 1927, Li Li-san [Li Lisan] from summer 1928 to summer 1930, and the International Faction (or the 28 Bolsheviks) from January 1931 to January 1935. (Ch'en 1986: 168–169)

This description shows frequent changes in the CCP leadership between 1927 and 1935. In the two years before the arrival of the '28 Bolsheviks' Li Lisan is said to have been Party leader. Ch'en provides no leader for the second half of 1930, thus indicating a power struggle. For the four-year rule of the '28 Bolsheviks', Ch'en gives precise dates for the beginning and end but does not mention any names.

It is also interesting to note what Jerome Ch'en does not write at this point. In the period discussed there was only one Party congress – the Sixth CCP Congress (July 1928). Following the defeats and persecutions of 1927 this congress was held in Moscow. Conforming to Comintern strategy a worker called Xiang Zhongfa – who is not mentioned in Chen's list – was made general secretary. The Standing Committee of the Politburo now included five full (Su Zhaozheng, Xiang Zhongfa, Xiang Ying, Zhou Enlai, Cai Hesen) and three alternate members (see Table 1).

Table 1: The Politburo after the First Plenum of the Sixth Central Committee (19 July 1928)

General secretary	Xiang Zhongfa
Politburo: *Standing Committee*	Members: Su Zhaozheng, Xiang Zhongfa, Xiang Ying, Zhou Enlai, Cai Hesen, Alternate members: Li Lisan, Xu Xigen, Yang Yin
Politburo: *members*	Su Zhaozheng, Xiang Ying, Zhou Enlai, Xiang Zhongfa, Qu Qiubai, Cai Hesen, Zhang Guotao
Politburo: *alternate members*	Guan Xiangying, Li Lisan, Luo Dengxian, Peng Pai, Yang Yin, Lu Futan, Xu Xigen

(Source: Ma Qibin 1991: 690)

A comparison of this table and later tables demonstrates that the Party leadership was affected by several important changes in a very short time. Most people mentioned above left the leadership within two or three years. By early 1930 Su Zhaozheng had died and Cai Hesen was excluded from the Politburo; he was replaced by Li Lisan who also took his seat in the Standing Committee. As Xiang Zhongfa turned out to be a weak leader, Li Lisan and Zhou Enlai were the most powerful men. In March 1930 Zhou Enlai went to Moscow, where Politburo members Qu Qiubai and Zhang Guotao were also living. (Li Ping 1989: 180) Thus Li Lisan gained a dominating position within a short time but was never made general secretary. However, when the first 'Bolsheviks' returned to China, Li Lisan was regarded as the Party leader (cf. Jerome Ch'en, above) and became the target of their attacks.

THE '28 BOLSHEVIKS' AND THEIR RETURN TO CHINA

Since the early 1950s, the '28 Bolsheviks' and particularly Chen Shaoyu (Wang Ming), Qin Bangxian (Bo Gu) and Zhang Wentian (Luo Fu) have played an important role in most Western and Taiwanese accounts of CCP history.

In 1952 Boyd Compton published one of the earliest Western descriptions of the rise of the '28 Bolsheviks' and argued:

> Wang [Ming] returned from Moscow schooling in 1930 with twenty-seven comrades. In January of the following year, he, Po Ku [Bo Gu], Lo Fu [Luo Fu], and Shen Tse-min [Shen Zemin] led the attack on Li Li-san and immediately assumed the leading positions in the Central Committee. They monopolised these posts from 1931 until the ascendancy of Chinese-trained leaders around Mao in 1935–37. (Compton 1952: xxxvii)

Hu Chi-hsi, an expert on military affairs living in France, provided a more recent example for this widespread argument:

> In the context of Stalin's takeover of the world communist movement, a group of Chinese students from Moscow's Sun Yat-sen University led by Chen Shaoyu [Wang Ming], Qin Bangxian and Zhang Wentian, went to Shanghai with the undissimulated task of seizing control of the Chinese Communist Party (CCP). Aided by Mif, director of the Chinese section in the Comintern's Far Eastern Department, who went with them to China, these 'returned' students from the Soviet Union, the 'Twenty-Eight Bolsheviks' as they were later called succeeded in liquidating the 'Li Lisan line' and then taking over the leadership of the CCP at the 4th plenum of the VIth Central Committee in January 1931. Immediately after, the Twenty-Eight Bolsheviks sought to impose their authority over the revolutionary bases then existing in China, particularly in the Soviets of Jiangxi, Eyuwan (Hubei–Henan–Anhui) and Xiangexi (west Hunan–Hubei). (Hu 1988: 159)

In the current edition of *The Rise of Modern China*, Immanuel Hsü writes:

> The party leadership now fell to Wang Ming and Po Ku [Bo Gu], who headed the 'international wing' of the CCP consisting of twenty-eight returned students who had studied at the Sun Yat-sen University at Moscow from 1926 to 1930. Returning

home in early 1930, they became known as the 'Twenty-eight Bolsheviks' and 'China's Stalin Section'. They took over the Politburo in January 1931, with the support of Mif, the Comintern representative. (Hsü 1995: 555)

Most accounts of these developments contain five major assumptions:

1. A group of '28 Bolsheviks', led by Wang Ming and Qin Bangxian, returned to China in the spring or summer of 1930.
2. The Comintern envoy Pavel Mif accompanied and supported the group.
3. At the Fourth Plenum of January 1931 the group took over the Party leadership in Shanghai.
4. Following their success in Shanghai the group tried to take over the leadership in the Central Soviet of Jiangxi.
5. After the execution of general secretary Xiang Zhongfa in June 1931, Wang Ming became his successor.

On the basis of recently published Chinese sources these statements will now be examined in detail.

Who were the '28 Bolsheviks'?

There is no conclusive answer to this question. Most Western authors who mention the '28 Bolsheviks' provide only six (or even fewer) names: Wang Ming (Chen Shaoyu), Qin Bangxian (Bo Gu), Zhang Wentian (Luo Fu), He Zishu, Wang Jiaxiang and Shen Zemin. (Schwartz 1951: 148; Hsiao 1961: 13; North 1963: 140, Ch'en 1967: 159; Thornton 1969: 119–20; Guillermaz 1972: 204; Levine 1992: 439f.) In 1966 John Rue still stated: 'No complete list of the 28 has ever been published.'(Rue 1966: 7). This shows that the scholars who discussed the activities and impact of the '28 Bolsheviks' in the 1950s and early 1960s were not clear on who belonged to this group.

This leads to the question when and how the story of the '28 Bolsheviks' entered Western historical writing. A close look at the earliest works mentioning the '28' shows that both Benjamin Schwartz (1951: 148ff.) and Robert North (1953/1963: 68) quote Li Ang's *Red Stage (Hongse wutai)*, published in 1942 in Chongqing; Schwartz and North also mention the same six names given above. Boyd Compton (1952) does not provide any source. Later publications, such as Hsiao (1961: 13), Ch'en (1967: 159) Thornton

(1969: 120), Wilson (1971: 286), Uhalley (1988: 256), give Schwartz, North, or Li Ang as their source and the same six (or fewer) 'Bolsheviks' are listed. North (1968), Guillermaz (1972), Ch'en (1986), Ladany (1988) and Yang (1990) do not mention their sources. This shows that nearly all Western accounts of the '28 Bolsheviks' are based on Li Ang's book.

According to Chen Yutang's biographical dictionary, Li was a former CCP member called Zhu Qihua, who turned Trotskyite and left the Party in 1929; in 1941 he was arrested by the KMT and died in prison in 1945. (Chen Yutang 1993: 154–155) If this is correct – there are no other biographical accounts of Li Ang – the author was not in Moscow when the 'Bolshevik' group was allegedly formed and had already left the CCP when the 'Bolsheviks' returned to China, 'took over' the leadership and 'clashed' with Mao. Li did not enter the Jiangxi Soviet and did not take part in the Long March. This indicates that Li could not have been a witness of most of the events he described. From the middle of the 1950s doubts concerning the reliability of his account were raised: Conrad Brandt, one of the editors of the first major collection of CCP documents (Brandt et al. 1952), characterised *Red Stage* as 'a chatty, highly personal volume, in many places of dubious accuracy' (Brandt 1958: 197); Hsüeh Chün-tu remarked in his bibliography on Chinese communism that 'the author's attitude is so bitter, so sarcastic, and his language is so violently distorted that his statements should be accepted only with great caution' (Hsüeh 1960: 17). Even Robert North, who repeatedly used and quoted the book, admitted: 'Li Ang, who is vague about dates and sequences, appears to confuse many aspects of the First All–China Soviet Congress (1931) with the Second All–China Soviet Congress (1934)' (North 1963: 157). These comments demonstrate that even in the 1950s serious doubts concerning the reliability of 1950s Li Ang's story of the '28 Bolsheviks' were expressed. Still, for several decades *Red Stage* exerted a tremendous influence on Western China studies. According to John Rue (1966: 361), Stanford University, where Robert North taught, owned an unpublished English translation of this book, which was used by numerous authors. (This may be the reason why they often only referred to the numbers of chapters and not to precise page numbers, as these would have been different in the original and translation.) However, even Li Ang, who was quoted by so many

Western scholars had not provided a full list of the '28 Bolsheviks' (Li Ang 1942).

Starting in 1965, four Chinese authors (in Taiwan, Hong Kong and North America) – Wang Chien-min (1965), Warren Kuo (1968), Sheng Yueh (1971) and Sima Lu (1979) – published different lists with 28 names. Table 2 shows that they agreed on 23 persons and every author added different other names.

Table 2: Different Lists of '28 Bolsheviks' [(f)=female]

Name	Alternative Names	Kuo	Sheng	Sima	Wang
Chen Changhao		x	x	x	x
Chen Shaoyu	Wan(g) Min(g)	x	x	x	x
Chen Weimin	Sha Kefu	x		x	
Chen Yuandao	Lie Fu	x	x	x	x
Du Ting					x
Du Zuoxiang (f)	Du Z(h)uo-qiang	x	x	x	x
Guo Miaogen				x	x
He Kequan	Kai Feng		x		
He Zishu		x	x	x	x
Li Yuanjie		x	x		
Li Zhusheng		x	x	x	x
Liu Qunxian (f)		x		x	
Meng Qingshu (f)		x	x	x	x
Qin Bangxian	Bo Gu	x	x	x	x
Shen Zemin		x	x	x	x
Shen Zhiyuan	Shen Guanlan	x			
Sheng Zhongliang	Sheng Yue(h)	x	x	x	x
Song Panmin	Song Panming		x		

Sun Jimin	Sun Jiming	x	x	x	x
Wang Baoli			x	x	x
Wang Jiaxiang	Wang Jiaqiang	x	x	x	x
Wang Shengdi		x	x	x	x
Wang Shengrong		x	x	x	x
Wang Xiu					x
Wang Yuncheng		x	x	x	x
Xia Xi		x	x	x	x
Xiao Tefu			x		
Xu Yixin		x			
Yang Shangkun		x	x	x	x
Yin Jian		x	x	x	x
Yuan Jiayong	Yuan Mengchao	x	x	x	x
Yun Yurong				x	x
Zhang Qinqiu (f)		x	x	x	x
Zhang Wentian	Luo Fu	x	x	x	x
Zhu Agen		x	x	x	x
Zhu Zishun (f)	Zhu Zichun	x	x	x	x

Sources: Kuo 1968: 234; Sheng 1971: 216; Sima 1979: 36; Wang 1965: 100

The list presented by Sheng Yueh seems to be the most convincing. In contrast to the three other authors, Sheng studied in Moscow, was a member of the group and knew all the 28 people involved. Only Sheng included He Kequan, who was one of the most important members of the group. The other authors, who had no personal knowledge of most of the '28', included persons who had not been to Moscow or left too early. None of the authors provided any sources. Therefore Sheng Yueh's list will be used for the following analysis. In the People's Republic of China no alternative lists of 'Bolsheviks' appeared, but a Chinese translation of Sheng Yueh's book with his list was printed in Beijing. Chen Xiuliang, a former student of Sun Yat-sen University, confirmed most of the names; but she had doubts concerning some women in the list, as they were not Party but only Youth League members and not very active. (Chen Xiuliang 1983: 63) It will be shown below that the five disputed members – with the exception of He Kequan – did not play an important role in CCP politics.

There is, however, another problem: the exact number of 'Bolsheviks'. Mao Zedong and other Chinese politicians and authors (Xie Yan 1995: 45) often repeatedly mentioned '28$^{1/2}$ Bolsheviks'. According to Sima Lu (1979: 36), Xu Yixin was described as the 'half Bolshevik', because he was very young and not a Party member. Warren Kuo (1968: 2/234) included Xu as a full member, other authors did not include him at all. Some authors write about 'Wang Ming and the 28 Bolsheviks' (see below), which would also mean 29 persons.

At this point, the origin of the term '28 Bolsheviks' must be considered. In June 1929 several hundred students of Sun Yat-sen University in Moscow participated in the so-called 'Ten Day Conference', only 28 were said to have voted for Stalin's and Pavel Mif's line (Sheng 1971: 218ff.; Cao Zhongbin 1988: 141ff.). If this frequently quoted account is correct, more than 28 people were involved, as Wang Ming [Chen Shaoyu] did not participate because he had already returned to China (see below). Wang Ming's own account clarifies the situation:

> The so-called 'Chen Shao-yu group' was invented by the Trotskyites and Chen Tu-hsiuists in the winter of 1927. [...] The tale of the '28$^{1/2}$ Bolsheviks' and the 'Chen Shao-yu group' was also bandied about by Trotskyites and Chen Tu-hsiuists in the autumn of 1929 during the Party purge at CUTC [Sun Yat-sen University]. I had left Moscow for home in the beginning of February. (Wang 1979: 126–127)

Sheng Yueh, a 'Bolshevik' who published his memoirs in 1971 in the United States (in English), explicitly confirmed the existence of the group and emphasized the role of Pavel Mif, Sun Yat-sen University's director:

16

Mif did not create the 28 Bolsheviks. But because of their outstanding performance in the struggle in Sun Yat-sen University, they came to Mif's attention as a disciplined force which could be useful to him. For these twenty-eight people became the enemy of all 'anti-Party' factions in Sun Yat-sen University. They were as a result, dubbed the 28 Bolsheviks, which implied that they were merely the tag-ends of the Russian Bolsheviks. [...] It was either my good fortune or my bad fortune to have been at Sun Yat-sen University at the time that the 28 Bolsheviks appeared, and to have been one of them. (Sheng 1971: 215–216)

It should be stressed that the term 'Bolsheviks' and the numbers '28', '28$^{1/2}$' and '29' appeared in Moscow in the late 1920s in connection with the factional fighting involving 'Trotskyites' and other groups. This had nothing to do with their return to China or later power struggles with Li Lisan or Mao Zedong. The 'Bolsheviks' were seen as a group in Moscow in 1928–29; thus, only people who were in Moscow during these years could identify the '28'. For a Chinese author who had not been to Moscow, it was not possible to identify them. Even for students in Moscow it was difficult, as many students used pseudonyms.

In the following chapters I shall use the term '28 Bolsheviks' for the 28 persons listed by Sheng Yueh (1971), who studied and co-operated in Moscow in the late 1920s. For the developments of the 1930s it is important to analyse if and for how long they can be considered as a group or faction.

In addition to the term '28 Bolsheviks', publications in Chinese and English have also included other terms, such as 'Internationalists' (guojipai), 'Wang Ming-faction' (Wang Ming pai) and 'Russian Returned Students' (liu E pai). The following quotes show that these were used as synonyms: 'The "Returned Student Clique" [...] known also among the party veterans by other ironic appellations such as the "Twenty-eight Bolsheviks"' (Schwartz 1951: 148). 'The returned-student group (the so-called 28 bolsheviks)' (Kim 1973: 56). 'This group, [...] called the Russian Returned Students, or the Twenty-Eight Bolsheviks' (Thornton 1982: 37). 'The International Faction (or the 28 Bolsheviks)' (Ch'en 1986: 168–169).

In Moscow the terms '28 Bolsheviks', 'Stalinists' and 'Wang Ming-group' made sense, the term 'Russian Returned Student' did

17

not make sense before their return. Hu Chi-hsi's description 'these "returned" students from the Soviet Union, the "Twenty-Eight Bolsheviks" as they were later called' (Hu 1988: 159) is misleading.

In the People's Republic of China, the terms '28 Bolsheviks' and 'Internationalists' were never officially used. In the 1950s open criticism of Stalin, the Comintern and the Soviet Union was avoided and for decades former 'Bolsheviks' occupied important leadership posts. In 1988 Yang Shangkun even became state president. Instead, rather general terms such as '"left" faction', '"left" group', '"left" deviation', '"left" line', '"left" doctrinaire-sectarian comrades', or 'Wang Ming-Faction' were used (Central Committee 1953: 174, 182–3; Hu 1951: 16ff.). The now well-known references to '28 Bolsheviks' and '28½ Bolsheviks' come from unedited speeches of Mao Zedong (see below), Red Guard publications and internal sources. However, since the late 1980s censorship activities could no longer prevent the use of the term, particularly in biographies and memoirs.

The regional and social background of the '28 Bolsheviks'

An important element in the 'story' of the '28 Bolsheviks' is the highlighting of their 'youth' and 'inexperience'. Schwartz (1951: 149), North (1963: 140) and Wilson (1971: 24) quote exactly the same translation of the same sentences from Li Ang's *Red Stage*:

> These fellows were all young students who, needless to say, had made no contribution whatsoever to the revolution. While we were carrying on the revolution they were still suckling at their mothers' breasts ... These men who were infants in terms of their revolutionary background were now sent back to be the leaders of the Chinese Revolution.

To prove or falsify this account it is obviously necessary to study their background and education in detail. Until the 1980s there were, however, not enough biographical sources on the '28 Bolsheviks' to do this kind of research. The biographical dictionaries published by Klein and Clark (1971), Boorman (1967ff.), Bartke (1985) and Lazitch and Drachkovitch (1986) did not include more than ten of the '28 Bolsheviks' and these entries were full of gaps and mistakes. Unfortunately Sheng Yueh (1971) did not provide detailed biographical data. This situation only improved in the middle of the 1980s with new publications from the People's

Republic of China. Now it is possible to find basic biographical data, including year and place of birth, on most of the 'Bolsheviks'.

The most important details concerning the background and early activities of the '28 Bolsheviks' will be given below. This list includes the main biographical sources which were also used for the following tables.

Chen Changhao was born in 1906 in Hanyang (Hubei). He studied in Wuchang and became active in the student movement. He joined the Youth League in July 1926 and the CCP in 1930 (Chen Yutang 1993: 513; Sheng Ping 1991: 462).

Chen Shaoyu was born on 9 April 1904 into a landlord family of Lu'an (Anhui). In 1924 he went to university in Wuchang, where he came into contact with communist teachers. In 1925 he joined the Youth league and, shortly afterwards, the CCP. In the 1930s he became famous under the pseudonym **Wang Ming** (in Western language Comintern publications also: Wan Min) (Cao Zhongbin 1991: 427f.; Zhou Guoquan 1990: 1ff.). I shall use the better-known name Wang Ming.

Chen Yuandao was born on 25 April 1901 into a peasant family of Chaoxian (Anhui). He went to school in Wuhu and participated in the student movement. He joined the Youth League in 1923 and the CCP in 1925 (Sheng Ping 1991: 467).

Du Zuoxiang was born in Hubei, married Chen Changhao in Moscow and later Sheng Zhongliang (Cao Zhongbin 1989: 4). Together with Meng Qingshu she worked as an interpreter at the CCP's Sixth Party congress (1928) (Sheng 1971: 190). According to a former student of Sun Yat-sen University, she did not engage in political activities (Chen Xiuliang 1983: 63).

He Kequan – better known as Kai Feng – was born on 2 February 1906 in Pingxiang (Jiangxi). This county borders on the province of Hunan and was an early centre of CCP activities. He grew up in a rich landlord family and in 1925 went to university in Wuchang. He already had contacts with communists when he was at school, joined the Youth League in 1927 and the CCP in 1930 (Yi Shaolin 1994: 167f.).

He Zishu was born in 1901 in Yingshan (Hubei), his father was an intellectual. He went to a college in Wuchang and had by 1925 joined the CCP and led a local party branch. When the Northern

Figure 2: Shen Zemin (*right*), Zhang Wentian (*centre*) and Shen's brother, the author Mao Dun (*left*), in 1920.

Expedition reached Wuchang, he joined the army (Hubei sheng Yingshan xianzhi bianzuan weiyuanhui 1990: 664).

Li Yuanjie was born in Sichuan (Cao Zhongbin 1989: 4).

Li Zhusheng was born around 1904 in Shouxian (Anhui) (Cao Zhongbin 1989: 5).

Meng Qingshu was born on 2 December 1911 in Shouxian (Anhui). She grew up in a landlord family. In Moscow she met Wang Ming who came from a neighbouring county. On 23 November 1930 they married in Shanghai (Cao Zhongbin 1991: 102; Zhou Guoquan 1990: 119).

Qin Bangxian was born on 24 June 1907 in Hangzhou; his father was an official and lawyer in Shanghai and Zhejiang. His family, which resided in Wuxi (Jiangsu) had produced numerous scholars, including several *juren* and *jinshi*. In 1925 Qin went to the 'leftist' Shanghai University, joined the Youth League and, in October, the CCP. In the 1930s he became famous as Bo Gu, which was a part of the Russian name he used at Sun Yat-sen University (Li Zhiying 1994: 3ff.).

Shen Zemin, a younger brother of the author and CCP functionary Shen Yanbing (Mao Dun), was born in 1902 in Tongxiang (Zhejiang). In 1920 he and Zhang Wentian (see below) spent

20

half a year in Japan and in 1921 Shen joined the CCP in Shanghai. In January 1922 he participated in the first Youth League congress and was elected to its Central Committee. In the following years he worked for several leftist journals and taught at Shanghai University (Chen Yutang 1993: 413; Sheng Ping 1991: 380).

Sheng Zhongliang, who published a book on Sun Yat-sen University (as Sheng Yueh), did not discuss his own background. He was born around 1905 in Liling (Hunan) and seems to have joined the CCP before his departure to Moscow (1926) (Cao Zhongbin 1989: 4). He had studied in Peking from 1923 to 1926 and worked in the local CCP propaganda department (Yao Weidou 1980: 815).

Song Panmin (Panming) was born into a working-class family in Wuhan (Hubei) or Henan and probably joined the CCP in 1927 (Sheng 1971: 241; Sheng Ping 1991: 389).

Sun Jimin was born around 1905 in Wuhan (Hubei) and joined the CCP in 1926 or 1927 (Cao Zhongbin 1989: 5; Shanghai Municipal Police: D4454).

Wang Baoli, was born in 1905 and came from a Nanjing (Jiangsu) working-class family (Cao Zhongbin 1989: 5; Sheng 1971: 47).

Wang Jiaxiang was born into a landlord family on 15 August 1906 in Jingxian (Anhui). He went to an English missionary school in Wuhu and, in September 1925, to the middle school of Shanghai University. In October he joined the Youth League and was selected for studying in Moscow (Wang Jiaxiang xuanji bianjizu 1985: 232).

Wang Shengdi was born around 1903 in Hunan, studied in Paris in the early 1920s and later moved to Moscow (Cao Zhongbin 1989: 5; Sheng 1971: 76).

Wang Shengrong was born around 1907 in Wuhan (Hubei) and was already a CCP member when he arrived in Moscow in 1927 (Wang Shengrong 1984: 22).

Wang Yuncheng was born around 1905 in Wuhan (Hubei). After four years at school he worked in several factories. In 1926 or 1927 he joined the CCP and – in late 1927 – went to Moscow (Cao Zhongbin 1989: 5; Shanghai Municipal Police: D4454).

Xia Xi was born in 1901 in Yiyang (Hunan) and well-educated. He went to a college in the provincial capital Changsha and met Mao Zedong. In 1920 Xia Xi joined the Youth League and, in

1921, the CCP. In the following winter he spent several weeks in the Soviet Union, but soon returned to Hunan. At the Fifth CCP congress of May 1927 Xia entered the Central Committee and was one of the most experienced and highest ranking 'Bolsheviks'. At the Sixth Party congress in 1928, he was however, not re-elected to the Central Committee (Liu Jintian 1992: 297; Sheng Ping 1991: 611).

Xiao Tefu was born 1903 in Taoyuan (Hunan) and studied in France before moving to Moscow (Cao Zhongbin 1989: 5; Sheng 1971: 76).

Yang Shangkun was born on 25 May 1907 in Tongnan, near Chongqing (Sichuan). He grew up in a big landlord family and, following his older brother Yang Angong, joined the Youth League in 1925 and the CCP in 1926. After Angong's arrest and execution in 1927, his friend Zhang Wentian supported Yang Shangkun. Zhang had worked in Chongqing as a teacher and taught Yang's future wife Li Bozhao, who also studied at Sun Yat-sen University in the late 1920s (Liu Jintian 1992: 126; Sheng Ping 1991: 265).

Yin Jian was born in 1903 or 1904 in Wuhan (Hubei). (Cao Zhongbin 1989: 4)

Yuan Jiayong was born in August 1905 in Ziyang (Sichuan) and went to university in Nanjing. He graduated in 1926 and joined the CCP on 17 July 1927 (Cao Zhongbin 1989: 3; Chen Rongfu 1990: 367).

Zhang Qinqiu was a daughter of a scholar and was born on 15 November 1904. She and Shen Zemin (see above) grew up in Tongxiang (Zhejiang) and married in 1924. From 1921 she studied at a college in Hangzhou. In 1924 she became a member of the Youth League and the CCP. Following Shen Zemin's death (in 1933) she lived with Chen Changhao (Xie Yan 1995: 1ff.).

Zhang Wentian was born on 30 August 1900 in Nanhui (Jiangsu) near Shanghai and was the oldest 'Bolshevik'. He grew up in a peasant family and in 1917 went to a technical school. From 1920 to 1924 he studied and worked in Tokyo and California. He was one of the few Chinese communists, who visited the United States before 1949. He published a novel and other texts

22

and worked as a teacher and editor. In June 1925 he joined the CCP in Shanghai. In the 1930s, he used the pseudonym Luo Fu, which was a part of the Russian name he used in Moscow (Cheng Zhongyuan 1993: 1ff.).

Zhu Agen was born into a Shanghai working-class family in 1904, and joined the CCP in the middle of the 1920s (Cao Zhongbin 1989: 4; Sheng 1971: 241ff.).

Zhu Zishun was a friend of Meng Qingshu. (Sheng 1971: 200) According to Chen Xiuliang, Meng and Zhu were not Party but only Youth League members when they studied in Moscow (Chen Xiuliang 1983: 63).

Table 3: Years of birth and home provinces of the '28 Bolsheviks'

Name	Alternative Names	Year of birth	Home Province	City / County
Chen Changhao		1906	Hubei	Hanyang
Chen Shaoyu	Wan(g) Min(g)	1904	Anhui	Lu'an
Chen Yuandao	Lie Fu	1901	Anhui	Chaoxian
Du Zuoxiang (f)	Du Zhuoqiang	19??	Hubei	
He Kequan	Kai Feng	1906	Jiangxi	Pingxiang
He Zishu		1901	Hubei	Yingshan
Li Yuanjie		190?	Sichuan	
Li Zhusheng		1904?	Anhui	Shouxian
Meng Qingshu (f)		1911	Anhui	Shouxian
Qin Bangxian	Bo Gu	1907	Jiangsu	Wuxi
Shen Zemin		1902	Zhejiang	Tongxiang
Sheng Zhongliang	Sheng Yue(h)	1905?	Hunan	Liling
Song Panmin	Song Panming	190?	?	
Sun Jimin		1905	Hubei	Wuhan
Wang Baoli		1905	Jiangsu	Nanjing
Wang Jiaxiang	Wang Jiaqiang	1906	Anhui	Jingxian

Wang Shengdi		1903	Hunan	
Wang Shengrong		1907?	Hubei	Wuhan
Wang Yuncheng		1905?	Hubei	Wuhan
Xia Xi		1901	Hunan	Yiyang
Xiao Tefu		1903	Hunan	Taoyuan
Yang Shangkun		1907	Sichuan	Tongnan
Yin Jian		1904?	Hubei	Wuhan
Yuan Jiayong	Yuan Mengchao	1905	Sichuan	Ziyang
Zhang Qinqiu (f)		1904	Zhejiang	Tongxiang
Zhang Wentian	Luo Fu	1900	Jiangsu	Nanhui
Zhu Agen		1904	Jiangsu	Shanghai
Zhu Zishun (f)	Zhu Zichun	?	?	

(Sources: see main text)

Most, if not all, 'Bolsheviks' were born between 1900 and 1911. They were only slightly younger than the above-mentioned CCP leaders Li Lisan (1899) and Qu Qiubai (1899) and about the same age as Peng Zhen (1902), Deng Xiaoping (1904), Chen Yun (1905) and – Li Ang (1907). The 'Bolsheviks' came from numerous provinces, including Hubei (7) Anhui (5), Hunan (4), Jiangsu (4), Sichuan (3) and Zhejiang (2); this shows that they did not come from the same region. They came from big cities (like Shanghai, Wuhan, Nanjing and Hangzhou) from small towns and villages. The 'Bolsheviks' grew up in landlord, worker and peasant families and did not share the same social background. Some had been to a university, others only to middle school; some could hardly read or write. Shen Zemin and Xia Xi joined the CCP in 1921 and belonged to its earliest members, others only joined the Party at the end of the decade. Shen Zemin, Zhang Wentian, Wang Shengdi and Xiao Tefu had already been abroad (Japan, France, USA) before travelling to Moscow, some of the others had not even left their home province.

This brief biographical survey contradicts Li Ang's claim of the youth and inexperience of the '28'. The biographies of the

'Bolsheviks' do not support the theory of 'homogeneity' of this group, often emphasized in Western accounts. Richard Kagan's description 'They were primarily the young, the super ideological, and those very inexperienced in Chinese political affairs' (Kagan 1974: 79–80) is not correct.

The '28 Bolsheviks' at Sun Yat-sen University

All the '28 Bolsheviks' studied at Moscow's Sun Yat-sen University. The establishment of this university and the visits of Trotsky and Stalin demonstrated Moscow's support for the First United Front of the KMT and CCP (1924–1927). In the autumn of 1925 – several months after Sun Yat-sen's death – the university was founded by Trotsky and headed by his supporter Karl Radek. After Radek's dismissal in 1927, Stalin's China-specialist Pavel Mif took over. The five-year history of Sun Yat-sen University was characterized by bitter struggles between students supporting Stalin and Trotsky, and between CCP and KMT supporters (who left in 1927 after the end of the First United Front). These struggles also caused the closure of the university in 1930 (Sheng 1971: 31ff.; Cao Zhongbin 1988: 13ff.).

Most students attended two-year courses, starting in autumn or early winter. Table 4 shows that the 'Bolsheviks' were not travelling there together and did not arrive in the same year, as some publications have suggested (Schwartz 1951: 148; Hsiao 1961: 12; Hsü 1995: 555). Six 'Bolsheviks' began in 1925, five in 1926, fifteen in 1927 and one in 1928; it is not known when Xiao Tefu started, he travelled from France to Moscow. In the first two years, when the First United Front was working well, both the CCP and Kuomintang carefully selected students to be sent to Moscow (including Chiang Kai-shek's son Chiang Ching-kuo and two sons of Feng Yuxiang) (Sheng 1971: 20ff.; Cao Zhongbin 1988: 20ff.). The first communist students left Shanghai on 28 October and reached Moscow on 23 November 1925. These included Wang Ming, Wang Jiaxiang, Zhang Wentian and Zhang Qinqiu (Cao Zhongbin 1991: 430). Together with Qin Bangxian, who joined in the following year, they later became the core of the '28 Bolsheviks'. After the breakup of the First United Front (1927), numerous communists fled to Moscow and became students of Sun Yat-sen University. At the same time, most KMT students returned to China. Because of the fighting in China, many communist students of the first two years could not return home after graduating and remained in Moscow as teachers, interpreters and translators; some became postgraduate students (Sheng 1971: 118ff.; Chen Xiuliang 1983: 44ff.)

Table 4: The arrival of the '28 Bolsheviks' in Moscow

Name	Year	Name	Year
Wang Ming	1925	He Zishu	1927
Chen Yuandao	1925	Meng Qingshu (f)	1927
Shen Zemin	1925	Song Panmin	1927
Wang Jiaxiang	1925	Sun Jimin	1927
Zhang Qinqiu (f)	1925	Wang Baoli	1927
Zhang Wentian	1925	Wang Shengdi	1927
Li Yuanjie	1926	Wang Shengrong	1927
Li Zhusheng	1926	Wang Yuncheng	1927
Qin Bangxian	1926	Yin Jian	1927
Sheng Zhongliang	1926	Yuan Jiayong	1927
Yang Shangkun	1926	Zhu Agen	1927
Chen Changhao	1927	Zhu Zishun (f)	1927
Du Zuoxiang (f)	1927	Xia Xi	1927–8
He Kequan	1927	Xiao Tefu	192?

(Source: Cao Zhongbin 1988: 26ff)

THE RETURN OF THE '28 BOLSHEVIKS'

The importance of the 'Comintern-co-ordinated' return of the '28 Bolsheviks' has often been emphasized in descriptions of factional fighting in the CCP leadership in the 1930s. In this context it has often been argued that they accompanied Stalin's China specialist Pavel Mif to Shanghai. In 1951, Benjamin Schwartz, in his first book on Mao Zedong, claimed:

> The '28 Bolsheviks' were 'Mif's protégés. Since Mif was at this time the most eminent Stalinist "China expert" his patronage was a matter of considerable weight. Thus we find that when Mif was appointed Comintern Delegate to China in the spring of 1930, his young protégés accompanied him back to China.' (Schwartz 1951: 148f.)

Two decades later the argument was quite similar. In the *Biographic Dictionary of Chinese Communism* we read:

> Li [Li-san's] activities in China were not favorably viewed in Moscow by Stalin and the Comintern; hence it was to counter Li that Mif and his '28 Bolsheviks' returned to China late in the spring of 1930. (Klein and Clark 1971: 195)

In the 1980s this was, as Thornton's survey of China's political history shows, still repeated:

> Moscow's reaction to Li [Lisan]'s policy was to send a carefully selected and loyal group of Chinese, then undergoing training at Moscow's Sun Yat-sen University, back to China in an effort to bring Li's policy into line. In the spring of 1930 this group, led by Ch'en Shao-yü (Wang Ming) and called the Russian Returned Students, or the Twenty-Eight Bolsheviks, returned to China. (Thornton 1982: 37)

According to the biographical sources available now, the return of the '28 Bolsheviks' started with Wang Ming and Chen Yuandao in early 1929, Meng Qingshu followed at the end of the year (Cao Zhongbin 1991: 103; Zhou Guoquan 1990: 51). In the spring of 1930 Wang Jiaxiang, He Zishu and Qin Bangxian returned. (Cao Zhongbin 1991:166) In late summer Shen Zemin travelled via France and shortly afterwards his wife Zhang Qinqiu via Siberia (Xie Yan 1995: 47). In autumn, Chen Changhao and Wang Shengrong arrived in Shanghai (Li Ping 1988: 8). Yang Shangkun and Zhang Wentian took the Transsiberian Railway and reached Shanghai on 17 February 1931 (Cheng Zhongyuan 1993: 118). He Kequan, Li Zhusheng, Wang Shengrong and Yin Jian returned in 1930, Wang

Baoli, Wang Yuncheng and Sun Jimin in 1931, Sheng Zhongliang and Wang Shengdi in 1932, Yuan Jiayong and Zhu Agen in 1933 (Cao Zhongbin 1989; Shanghai Municipal Police Files: D4454; Yuan Mengchao 1984: 3).

Table 5 indicates, that the return of the '28 Bolsheviks' took five years (1929–33) and that a 'co-ordination' of the return of more than three or four persons is unlikely. There was certainly no co-ordinated return of all 28 persons. Four 'Bolsheviks', who wanted to return to China much earlier (Sheng Zhongliang, Sun Jimin, Wang Shengdi and Yuan Jiayong) were forced to work in East Siberia in 1931 and 1932 before receiving approval to leave the Soviet Union (Sheng 1971: 237). The assumption that all 28 Bolsheviks were sent home together to overthrow Li Lisan is completely wrong. The main reason for the return of numerous students (of all factions and persuasions) from 1930 was simply the closure of Sun Yat-sen University in that year.

Table 5: The return of the '28 Bolsheviks' to China

Name	Year
Wang Ming	March 1929
Chen Yuandao	spring 1929
Meng Qingshu (f)	early 1930
Wang Jiaxiang	spring 1930
He Zishu	spring 1930
Qin Bangxian	May 1930
Shen Zemin	summer 1930
Li Yuanjie	summer–autumn 1930
Li Zhusheng	summer–autumn 1930
Wang Shengrong	summer–autumn 1930
Chen Changhao	autumn 1930
Xia Xi	autumn 1930

Zhang Qinqiu (f)	autumn 1930
He Kequan	autumn 1930
Du Zuoxiang (f)	1930
Song Panmin	1930/31
Zhang Wentian	February 1931
Yang Shangkun	February 1931
Yin Jian	early 1931
Sun Jimin	1931
Wang Yuncheng	1931
Wang Baoli	1931?
Wang Shengdi	1932?
Yuan Jiayong	early 1933
Sheng Zhongliang	early 1933
Zhu Agen	1933?
Xiao Tefu	193?
Zhu Zishun (f)	193?

(Sources: see main text)

The following paragraph shows that the '28 Bolsheviks' returned to a very dangerous city, in which they – and other communists – always risked arrest and execution. Some of them soon left Shanghai and took up responsibilities in other provinces.

On 12 January 1930 Wang Ming was arrested and, on 18 February, released. His girlfriend, Meng Qingshu, was arrested on 30 July and released on 22 November (Zhou Guoquan 1990: 119). On 17 December 1930 Li Yuanjie was arrested; He Kequan was sent to Hong Kong in the spring of 1931 and detained in May; after his release in October he returned to Shanghai (Yi Shaolin 1994: 169ff.). He Zishu, Yin Jian and Wang Baoli were arrested in 1931 or 1932, He Zishu is said to have died in a Peking Prison in 1932, Yin Jian in 1937 (Wang

1979: 15, 153). Other people arrested in Shanghai include Wang Shengdi in December 1932, Wang Yuncheng and Sun Jimin in February 1933, Li Zhusheng, Yuan Jiayong and Du Zuoxiang in June 1934 and Sheng Zhongliang in October 1934. (Kuo 1968: 2/313ff.) Chen Yuandao went to Tianjin in January 1931, was arrested in April of that year and released in September 1932; he was rearrested in January 1933 and, on 10 April 1933, executed in Nanjing (Sheng Ping 1991: 467).

Between the spring of 1931 and the spring of 1933 Wang Jiaxiang, He Kequan, Yang Shangkun, Zhang Wentian and Qin Bangxian went to the Central Soviet. In the spring of 1931 Shen Zemin, Zhang Qinqiu and Chen Changhao went to the Hubei, Henan and Anhui (E–Yu–Wan) border area, where Shen died on 20 November 1933 (Liu Jintian 1992: 183; Sheng Ping 1991: 380ff.). In 1931 Song Panmin and Xia Xi went to the Westhubei–Hunan–Base (Xiang–E–xi), where, in November 1933, Song Panmin was executed following an argument with Xia Xi; Xia Xi was killed in a battle on 28 February 1936 (Sheng Ping 1991: 389, 611). In October 1931 Wang Ming and Meng Qingshu left China for Moscow (Cao Zhongbin 1991: 237).

A comparison of Table 5 about the return of the '28 Bolsheviks' with Table 6 showing their later fate indicates that the '28' never stayed at the same place in China and never acted together. When the last 'Bolsheviks' returned from the Soviet Union in 1933 and

Table 6: The fate of the '28 Bolsheviks' (1930–36)

Name	Date	Event
Wang Ming	January 1930	arrested, released in February
Meng Qingshu	July 1930	arrested, released in November
Li Yuanjie	December 1930	arrested
Xia Xi	March 1931	transferred to Xiang–E–xi area, killed on 28 February 1936
Wang Jiaxiang	March 1931	transferred to Central Soviet
Shen Zemin	April 1931	transferred to E–Yu–Wan area, died on 20 November 1933

Zhang Qinqiu (f)	April 1931	transferred to E–Yu–Wan area
Chen Changhao	April 1931	transferred to E–Yu–Wan area
Chen Yuandao	April 1931	arrested, released in 1932
He Kequan	spring 1931	transferred to Hong Kong, imprisoned for three months
Wang Ming	October 1931	transferred to Moscow
Meng Qingshu (f)	October 1931	transferred to Moscow
Wang Baoli	1931	arrested
Yin Jian	1931	arrested, died after release in 1937
Wang Shengrong	1931	transferred to Central Soviet
Song Panmin	1931	transferred to Xiang–E–xi area, executed in 1933
He Zishu	1932	arrested, killed
Yang Shangkun	autumn 1932	transferred to Central Soviet
Wang Shengdi	December 1932	arrested
Zhang Wentian	December 1932	transferred to Central Soviet
Qin Bangxian	January 1933	transferred to Central Soviet
Chen Yuandao	January 1933	arrested, executed on 10 April 1933
Sun Jimin	February 1933	arrested
Wang Yuncheng	February 1933	arrested
He Kequan	spring 1933	transferred to Central Soviet
Zhu Agen	1933	arrested
Du Zuoxiang (f)	June 1934	arrested
Yuan Jiayong	June 1934	arrested
Li Zhusheng	June 1934	arrested
Sheng Zhongliang	October 1934	arrested

(Sources: Kuo 1968: 2/313ff.; Sheng Ping 1991)

1934, some who had returned earlier – He Zishu and Chen Yuandao – were already dead. Some of the survivors were in Kuomintang and warlord prisons, others went to other provinces in the North, West and South.

THE FIRST CONFRONTATION WITH LI LISAN

Wang Ming's departure from the Soviet Union and his arrival in Shanghai in early 1929 has hardly been noticed by Western scholars. This is partly due to the fact that Wang did not belong to the Party leadership and was not in a position to influence it. After Wang was arrested on 12 January 1930 (and released five weeks later), the Party leadership criticised his behaviour. Following that, Wang wrote a letter to Pavel Mif in Moscow, criticising the CCP leadership (Sheng 1971: 236; Cao Zhongbin 1991: 434–435).

Shortly after that, three other 'Bolsheviks' left Moscow for China. In March Wang Jiaxiang and He Zishu returned. Two months later Qin Bangxian and his wife, Liu Qunxian, followed (Li Zhiying 1994: 68).

On 9 July, shortly after the arrival of Qin Bangxian, Wang Jiaxiang and He Zishu, there was a controversy between the four 'Bolsheviks' and Li Lisan. They criticised the Central Committee Resolution of 11 June 1930 *The new revolutionary rising tide and preliminary successes in one or more provinces* (Brandt 1952: 179ff.). This first clash was a clear defeat for the four 'Bolsheviks' involved. Wang Ming and Qin Bangxian were reprimanded, Wang Jiaxiang was sent to Hong Kong and He Zishu to Tianjin. For the following six months the 'Bolsheviks' were excluded from the Party leadership (Cao Zhongbin 1991: 163ff.; Li Zhiying 1994: 73ff.).

ZHOU ENLAI, QU QIUBAI AND THE THIRD PLENUM

Li Lisan's policies and, particularly the decision of 11 June, provoked growing opposition by the Comintern in Moscow. On 16 July, the situation in China was discussed and on 23 July the Executive Committee of the Comintern passed a decision criticising Li Lisan's strategy. In early August, CCP Politburo members Zhou Enlai and Qu Qiubai were sent from Moscow to Shanghai to push through Comintern policies. On 19 August Zhou Enlai reached Shanghai and, in the following days, attended several Politburo meetings. Qu Qiubai arrived in Shanghai at about the same time (Li Ping 1989: 182–189; Yang Yunruo 1988: 261–271).

Figure 3: Zhou Enlai (*front row: fourth from left*), Nie Rongzhen (*front row: first from left*) and Deng Xiaoping (*back row: third from right*) in France (1924). In the 1930s all of them participated in the Long March and the Zunyi Conference. In the 1960s they were all Politburo members. Li Fuchun (*front row: sixth from left*) and

Zhang Guotao who lived in Moscow in 1930 commented on the relationship between the Comintern and Zhou Enlai:

> The Comintern pinned its hopes on Chou En-lai and looked on Li Li-san as a mere braggart. Chou, by contrast, held real power and could influence Li Li-san's actions. [...] The Comintern treated him with great kindness. Stalin appreciated him very much, praising his consistently fine record in handling military and intelligence work. [...] What the Comintern hoped to achieve through him was for Chou En-lai to subtly change Li Li-san's deviations and shoulder the responsibilities of practical leadership of the CC of the CCP. Never once did Chou show a wavering attitude, which made the Comintern trust him all the more. (Chang 1972: 127)

In September 1930, the Third Plenum of the Sixth CC was convened. If all the '28 Bolsheviks' had, as many Western scholars claimed, already returned to China, they – or some of them – could have attended the Plenum (with or without Mif). Some scholars have, in fact, argued that the 'Bolsheviks' attended:

> August–September (1930): Third Plenum of CC, CCP, convenes in Lushan. Li Li-san [Li Lisan] is criticised by group led by Ch'en Shao-yu [Wang Ming] for his 'putschist' policy. (Brandt 1952: 35)

The *Biographic Dictionary of Chinese Communism* claims:

> The '28 Bolsheviks' attended the Third CCP Plenum called by Chü Ch'iu-pai [Qu Qiubai] and Chou En-lai [Zhou Enlai] at Lushan. (Klein 1971: 196)

According to the currently available above-mentioned sources, only about ten of the '28 Bolsheviks' had returned to China by September 1930. However, none of them attended the Third Plenum. The four who were punished in July, were not allowed to attend meetings of the Party leadership, and the others were not important enough to participate in a CC plenum. Table 7 gives the names of all participants of this meeting, which was held from 24 to 28 September in Shanghai (not Lushan).

The participants of the Third Plenum criticised Li Lisan but did not decide on a substantially different policy and did not dismiss Li Lisan. There were no dramatic changes in the leadership (see Table 8). Li Lisan, general secretary Xiang Zhongfa, Xiang Ying, Qu

Table 7: Participants of the Third Plenum (September 1930)

CC: Members	Xiang Zhongfa, Xu Xigen, Zhang Jinbao, Luo Dengxian, Zhou Enlai, Xiang Ying, Yu Maohuai, Qu Qiubai, Li Lisan, Gu Shunzhang
CC: Alternate members	Wang Fengfei, Shi Wenbin, Zhou Xiuzhu, Luo Zhanglong
Other participants	Ruan Xiaoxian, Zhang Kundi, He Chang, Chen Yu, Deng Fa, Li Weihan, Lin Yuying, Chen Yun, Wang Kequan, Li Fuchun, Wen Yucheng, Yuan Binghui, Lu Dingyi, Hu Junhe, Wu Zhenpeng, Nie Rongzhen, Pan Wenyou, Deng Yingchao

Note: '28 Bolsheviks' = **bold**
(Source: Jiang Huaxuan 1991: 116)

Qiubai, Zhou Enlai and Zhang Guotao (in Moscow) continued as members of the Politburo. But as Politburo members Qu Qiubai and Zhou Enlai had returned to China from Moscow there was a shift of power, particularly because Li Lisan had profited from Zhou Enlai's absence. At the Third Plenum, Wen Yucheng, Li Weihan, Chen Yu, Xu Binggen, Lu Wenzhi, He Chang and Deng Fa became new members and Yuan Binghui, Chen Yun, Lin Yuying, Wang Kequan, Zhu De, Huang Ping, Yun Daiying and Chen Tanqiu new alternate members of the Central Committee, but none of the '28 Bolsheviks' was included. Until the end of 1930 they were not represented in the Party leadership at all (Ma Qibin 1991: 690; Liu Jintian 1992: 2).

Table 8: The Party leadership after the Third Plenum

General secretary	Xiang Zhongfa
Politburo: members	Xiang Zhongfa, Xiang Ying, Zhou Enlai, Qu Qiubai, Li Lisan, Guan Xiangying, Zhang Guotao
Politburo: alternate members	Luo Dengxian, Xu Xigen, Lu Futan, Wen Yucheng, Li Weihan, Gu Shunzhang, Mao Zedong

Note: '28 Bolsheviks' = **bold**
(Sources: Jiang Huaxuan 1991: 119; Ma Qibin 1991: 690)

As the Third Plenum did not lead to significant changes, the Comintern leadership in Moscow took more drastic steps. In October a critical letter was sent to the Chinese Party leadership; it arrived on 16 November and was discussed in the Politburo two days later. Li Lisan was called to Moscow to report to the Comintern and left within a few days. Thus, the main enemy of the '28 Bolsheviks' was removed from the CCP leadership by the Comintern without the involvement of the 'Bolsheviks' (Li Ping 1989: 190–196; Tang Chunliang 1989: 135–136).

Summary

Recent Chinese publications and, particularly, biographies of Chinese communists contradict most Western assumptions concerning the '28 Bolsheviks'. The '28 Bolsheviks' were not a homogeneous group: they came from different provinces and all sections of the population, and differed in age, education and political experience. Recent biographies also show that there was no organised return of Pavel Mif and the '28 Bolsheviks' in the spring or summer of 1930. The return took about five years: Wang Ming left Moscow already in early 1929, and the very last 'Bolshevik' did not arrive in China until 1933.

The story of the '28 Bolsheviks' had always been riddled with contradictions: on the one hand it emphasized the strength of the Communist International and its determination to subjugate the Chinese Communist Party. On the other hand there was no convincing explanation for the half-year delay between the alleged return of Mif and the '28 Bolsheviks' in the spring of 1930 and their political 'takeover' at the CCP's Fourth Plenum in January 1931. Events related to the Third Plenum in September 1930 were among the weakest parts of the story. If Mif and his supporters had indeed arrived in China by that time, they could have attended and influenced its outcome – hence no Fourth Plenum would have been necessary. But, in fact, Mif and most of the 'Bolsheviks' did not arrive in China until after September 1930.

The reasons for and timing of the alleged dispatch of the '28 Bolsheviks' by the Comintern have never been fully explained. It has often been argued that the Comintern opposed Li Lisan's activities of June and July 1930. However, by that time several leading 'Bolsheviks', including Wang Ming himself, had already returned to

China, which shows that their decision to return was made earlier. In addition, supporters of the 'Bolshevik' story have failed to explain why Moscow should choose young, inexperienced students who were not Politburo or Central Committee members to overthrow Li Lisan. The Comintern's reaction to developments in China in the summer of 1930 was, in fact, the dispatch of Politburo members Qu Qiubai and Zhou Enlai who attended the Third Plenum.

Li Lisan's expulsion from the Politburo and his trip to Moscow were the results of direct Comintern intervention and did not involve the '28 Bolsheviks'.

Many Western accounts incorporate far-reaching conclusions based on a small number of extremely unreliable sources. The main source for the story of the '28 Bolsheviks' was Li Ang's *Red Stage*. The author had not been in Moscow when the '28 Bolsheviks' were studying there and was not a personal witness to the developments of 1930, a time when he had, in fact, already left the CCP. However, Li Ang's description of the '28 Bolsheviks' had a dramatic impact on Western research in the 1950s and was still repeated in the 1990s.

TWO

The Evolution of a New Party Leadership (1931)

Following the account of the return and early unsuccessful activities of the '28 Bolsheviks' given above, their so-called 'takeover' in 1931 will be discussed in this chapter. For more than half a century, the Fourth Plenum of the Sixth Central Committee was described as the beginning of the rule of Wang Ming and the '28 Bolsheviks'. Pavel Mif, who represented the Comintern at the Plenum, published the following account:

> A fight against Li Li-san's semi-Trotskyist policy was started in the Shanghai section of the Party under the leadership of Chen Shao-yu (Wang Ming). This fight for a correct line was quite successful. [...] It was only at the Fourth Enlarged Plenum of the Central Committee, held in January 1931, that the political line of the Party leadership was straightened out. The Fourth Plenum elected a new party leadership, exposed the anti-Leninist character of Li Li-san's policy and repelled the attempt of right opportunists to impose a defeatist programme of retreat upon the Party. In doing this the Fourth Plenum played an extremely important part in the further Bolshevisation of the party. (Miff 1937: 70–71)

The Central Committee *Resolution on some questions in the history of Our Party* argues that after 1927 the Party committed several mistakes:

> The gravest of all was the 'Left' deviation in the political, military and organisational lines in the period from the Central Committee's plenary session in January 1931 to the enlarged

meeting of the Central Political Bureau in January 1935. (Central Committee 1953: 174.)

This session, accomplishing nothing positive or constructive, accepted the new 'Left' line, which triumphed in the central leading body; thus began, for the third time during the Agrarian Revolutionary War, the domination of a 'Left' line in the Party. (Central Committee 1953: 182.)

This interpretation has not only dominated Chinese history writing for several decades; it also had a great impact on Western scholarship. In the *Cambridge History of China*, Jerome Ch'en still defined the period between January 1931 and January 1935 as the rule of the '28 Bolsheviks' (Ch'en 1986: 168–169).

In this chapter the Fourth Plenum will be discussed. The analysis of the months following the Plenum will also show that the above-mentioned Chinese and Western accounts do not adequately reflect the complicated developments of that period.

THE ARRIVAL OF THE COMINTERN REPRESENTATIVE PAVEL MIF IN SHANGHAI

The arrival of the Comintern's 'China specialist' Pavel Mif – together with the 'Bolsheviks' – has frequently been featured in Western China studies; but the date suggested was never correct. In 1951, Benjamin Schwartz argued:

> Thus we find that when Mif was appointed Comintern delegate to China in the spring of 1930, his young protégés accompanied him back to China. (Schwartz 1951: 149)

In the chronology of his impressive collection of communist documents, Hsiao Tso-liang also claimed:

> May or early June 1930: Pavel Mif arrives in China as Comintern delegate, bringing with him a group of his protégés popularly known as the Russian Returned Students. (Hsiao 1961: 307–8)

Even in the 1980s, when numerous new sources were available, Jürgen Domes still repeated this interpretation:

> The 'bolsheviks' had arrived in China with the new Comintern representative of the CCP Central Committee, Pavel Mif. (Domes 1985: 33)

Similar descriptions were published by Rue (1966: 348ff.), Klein and Clark (1971: 195) and Hu (1988: 159).

The above-mentioned arrests and executions have already indicated that a journey of a Soviet citizen with 28 Chinese communists would have been extremely dangerous and unthinkable. And Mif did not arrive in Shanghai in the spring, but in December 1930, between the Third and Fourth plenary sessions. If he had arrived in summer, he could and would have attended the Third Plenum in September. One reason for his arrival seems to have been the lack of a policy change at the Third Plenum of September. His trip followed several Comintern directives and Zhou Enlai's and Qu Qiubai's mission to China and was just one of several Comintern measures to direct and control CCP policy and activities (Yang Yunruo 1988: 281; Li Ping 1989: 197).

Even before Mif's arrival, Li Lisan had been ordered to go to Moscow. Li is said to have left Shanghai in the last week of November or early December and reported to the Comintern leadership later in December (Tang Chunliang 1989: 136ff.; Li Ping 1989: 195). Thus the main enemy of the '28 Bolsheviks' had already been removed. In the second week of December, Pavel Mif arrived in Shanghai (Yang Yunruo 1988: 281). Even though both dates are very close, there is no indication of a meeting of the two men. It is not known if the CCP leadership or the '28 Bolsheviks' knew about Mif's arrival in advance.

On 9 December, the Politburo passed a resolution criticising the resolution of 11 June and the Third Plenum. On 14 December Mif informed the Politburo about recent Comintern decisions. On 16 December the Politburo decided to repeal the punishment of Wang Ming, Qin Bangxian, He Zishu and Wang Jiaxiang of July 1930. This shows that the Comintern representative Pavel Mif and not the '28 Bolsheviks' enforced changes in CCP politics (Yang Yunruo 1988: 281; Li Ping 1989: 198).

THE FOURTH PLENUM AND CHANGES IN THE PARTY LEADERSHIP IN JANUARY 1931

Since the 1950s, the Fourth Plenum of the Sixth Central Committee in January 1931 has often been described as the date of Li

Lisan's defeat and the takeover by the '28 Bolsheviks'. This created the impression that the '28 Bolsheviks' attacked and overthrew Li Lisan at the Fourth Plenum. In 1952 Boyd Compton had argued:

Wang [Ming] returned from Moscow schooling in 1930 with twenty-seven comrades. In January of the following year, he [...] led the attack on Li Li-san and immediately assumed the leading positions in the Central Committee. (Compton 1952: xxxvii)

More than three decades later Jürgen Domes still claimed:

At the Fourth Plenum [...] Li was accused of 'leftist adventurism', relieved of all his posts in the Party, and sent to the Soviet Union 'for study'. The official Party leadership was thus taken over by the 'internationalist' pro-Comintern group, which was soon joined by Chou En-lai [Zhou Enlai], previously an ardent supporter of Li. (Domes 1985: 33–34)

Table 9: Participants of the Fourth Plenum (7 January 1931)

CC: Members	Xiang Zhongfa, Guan Xiangying, Wen Yucheng, Ren Bishi, He Chang, Li Wei-han, Yu Fei, Xu Xigen, Qu Qiubai, Luo Dengxian, Zhang Jinbao, Gu Shunzhang, Chen Yu, Zhou Enlai
CC: alternate members	Yuan Binghui, Chen Yun, Shi Wenbin, Zhou Xiuzhu, Luo Zhanglong, Wang Fengfei, Wang Kequan, Xu Lanzhi
Other participants:	Gu Zuolin, **Xia Xi, Chen Yuandao, Wang Jiaxiang, Wang Ming, Qin Bangxian**, Shen Xianding, He Mengxiong, **Shen Zemin**, Han Lianhui, Qiu Panlin, Xu Weisan, Ke Qingshi, Xiao Daode, Yuan Naixiang
Comintern representative	Pavel Mif

Note: '28 Bolsheviks' = **bold**
(Source: Jiang Huaxuan 1991: 125)

It has already been shown that one month before the Plenum, Li Lisan had already left for Moscow. It has also been indicated that in January 1931 many 'Bolsheviks' were still in the Soviet Union. Table 9 shows, that the '28 Bolsheviks' did not represent a majority of the participants. Only six were present: Wang Ming, Chen Yuandao, Qin Bangxian, Shen Zemin, Wang Jiaxiang and Xia Xi; they constituted only one fifth of the participants. (Zhang Wentian and Yang Shangkun only arrived a few weeks later.) Before the Plenum, none of the '28' was a member or alternate member of the Politburo or Central Committee.

Western accounts of the Fourth Plenum often emphasized the promotion of the '28 Bolsheviks' to the Central Committee and Politburo. In the 1960s, John Rue simply stated: 'Having placed the 28 Bolsheviks in the Politburo, Mif returned to Moscow.'(Rue 1966: 244) In the 1990s, June T. Dreyer claimed: 'At this point formal leadership of the CCP Central Committee passed to a group of people known as the "Returned Student" group or as the "Twenty-Eight Bolsheviks"'. (Dreyer 1993: 86)

Most recently, Stuart Schram argued that the Fourth Plenum

> finally and definitively repudiated the Li Lisan line and installed a new leading group headed by Chen Shaoyu (better known under his pseudonym, Wang Ming). Zhou Enlai [...] remained a member of the Politburo chosen at the Fourth Plenum. [...] Otherwise, the leadership was entirely made up of Mif's pupils and protégés known as the 'Twenty-eight Bolsheviks'. (Schram 1995: lxii)

Newly available sources, which were used for Table 10, show that the '28' had no majority in the Politburo or Central Committee, they were not even a strong minority. Only Wang Ming entered the Politburo, but not its Standing Committee. Richard Kagan's claim, that 'he became Secretary General of the Party [...] at the 4th Plenum' (Kagan 1974: 80) is not correct. Just two others, Shen Zemin and Xia Xi, became alternate members of the Central Committee. The three other 'Bolsheviks' who had been criticised in the preceding summer (He Zishu, Qin Bangxian and Wang Jiaxiang) and those who had returned in autumn and winter did not enter the Central Committee or Politburo.

Table 10: The Party leadership after the Fourth Plenum

General secretary:	Xiang Zhongfa
Politburo: Standing committee members	Xiang Zhongfa, Zhou Enlai, Zhang Guotao
Politburo: members	Xiang Zhongfa, Xiang Ying, Xu Xigen, Zhang Guotao, Chen Yu, Zhou Enlai, Lu Futan, Ren Bishi, **Wang Ming**
Politburo: alternate members	Luo Dengxian, Guan Xiangying, Wang Kequan, Liu Shaoqi, Wen Yucheng, Mao Zedong, Gu Shunzhang
CC: members	around 30, including: **Wang Ming**
CC: alternate members	around 17, including: **Shen Zemin, Xia Xi**

Note: '28 Bolsheviks' = **bold**
(Sources: Jiang Huaxuan 1991: 126; Ma Qibin 1991: 690; Liu Jintian 1992: 2)

In the reorganised leadership Zhou Enlai's position as one of only three members of the Standing Committee of the Polit-buro was very strong, because Xiang Zhongfa was a weak general secretary and Zhang Guotao had not returned from the Soviet Union. Zhou was an early member of the CCP and had participated in communist activities in Tianjin, Shanghai, Guangzhou and Wuhan. In addition, he had worked and studied in Japan, France, Germany, Great Britain and the Soviet Union, and spoke several foreign languages. As a leading participant in the Northern Expedition and the Nanchang Uprising he had also gained considerable military experience and knew most of the CCP's army leaders. He had been a Central Committee, Politburo and Standing Committee mem-ber since 1927, head of the CCP's Organisation Department since 1928 (see Kampen 1993: 301ff.) and head of the Central Military Commission since 1929 and was thus also heading the CCP's secret service. (Sheng Ping 1991: 525)

ARRESTS, EXECUTIONS, EXPULSIONS AND THEIR IMPACT

Most of the changes in the leadership in the first half of 1931 were not a result of the Fourth Plenum, but were due to expulsions, arrests and executions of senior communists. Denunciations may have played a role in the arrests, but are difficult to prove. The transfer of leading communists to different base areas led to further changes in the Party leadership.

In January 1931, many of those who opposed Mif and the '28 Bolsheviks', were expelled from the Party (Luo Zhanglong) or Central Committee (Wang Kequan and Wang Fengfei). He Mengxiong, Lin Yunan, Li Qiushi and other communists were arrested in the same month and, on 7 February, executed by the Kuomintang (Ma Qibin 1991: 231–232; Li Zhiying 1994: 94–95; Kuo 1968: 215ff.). The security chief Gu Shunzhang was arrested in April and general secretary Xiang Zhongfa on 22 June – two days later he was executed (Ma Qibin 1991: 239–242; Kuo 1968: 313). In March Ren Bishi and Gu Zuolin left for the Central Soviet (Zhang Xuexin 1994: 163–166), in April Zhang Guotao went to the E–Yü–Wan–Base in Northern Hubei and in June Li Weihan and Chen Yu went to Moscow (Li Weihan 1986: 331). Thus, by July 1931, many opponents of the '28 Bolsheviks' had left Shanghai and the Party Centre. Table 11 shows the most important cases.

Table 11: Expulsions from the CCP, arrests, executions and departures of leading CCP members from Shanghai

Name	Date	Event
Xiang Ying (PBM)	December 1930	transferred to Central Soviet
Wang Kequan (PBAM), Wang Fengfei (CCM), Luo Zhanglong (CCAM), Shi Wenbin (CCAM)	January 1931	expelled from CCP
He Mengxiong, Lin Yunan, Li Qiushi	January 1931	arrested and executed in February

Ren Bishi (PBM), Gu Zuolin	March 1931	transferred to Central Soviet
Zhang Guotao (PBM)	April 1931	transferred to Northern Hubei
Gu Shunzhang (PBAM)	April 1931	arrested
Chen Yu (PBM), Li Wei-han	June 1931	transferred to Moscow
Xiang Zhongfa (PBM, general secretary)	June 1931	arrested and executed
Guan Xiangying (PBAM)	August 1931	arrested
Zhou Enlai (PBM)	December 1931	transferred to Central Soviet
Wen Yucheng (PBAM)	January 1932	expelled from CCP
Xu Xigen (PBM), Yu Fei	September 1932	arrested
Lu Futan (PBM)	January 1933	arrested
Luo Dengxian (PBAM)	March 1933	arrested and executed

Note: '28 Bolsheviks' not included
(Sources:(Sources see main text)

WANG MING AND THE ESTABLISHMENT OF A NEW PROVISIONAL PARTY LEADERSHIP

Following the reduction of the number of Politburo members because of arrests, expulsions and departures, the influence of the remaining members grew rapidly. At the same time, because of the dangerous conditions, the activities of the Party leadership were also reduced. After Xiang Zhongfa's arrest, Zhou Enlai, Lu Futan and Wang Ming were the leading members of the Party (Li Ping 1989: 210–213; Li Zhiying 1994: 94–95). Western scholars have repeatedly claimed that Wang was promoted to general secretary in the summer of 1931:

> June [1931]: Hsiang Chung-fa arrested and executed. Wang Ming becomes Secretary of CCP Central Committee (Rue 1966: 350).

> Wang Ming, the Party's General Secretary since summer 1931 returned to Moscow (Heinzig 1971: 277).

> Wang Ming 'replaced Li Lisan as general secretary (*sic!*) of the party at age twenty-nine (*sic!*) and remained in power from 1931 to 1935'. (Apter 1995: 219)

Many other scholars mention the promotion of Wang Ming to general secretary in 1931, e.g. Bartke (1985: 32) and Dressler (1990: 262). But they do not provide any sources or precise dates. No CCP document with this information has been found. In the summer of 1931 there was no Party congress, no Central Committee Plenum and no important conference which could have made that decision. Following the above-mentioned arrests, Wang Ming, who had been in prison in 1930, and Zhou Enlai went into hiding and made preparations for their departure from Shanghai.

Wang Ming left Shanghai in October and spent the following six years in Moscow. In September 1931, Wang's close friend, Qin Bangxian, was appointed head of a provisional Party leadership (see Table 12), which also included the 'Bolsheviks' Zhang Wentian and Li Zhusheng, as well as Lu Futan, Kang Sheng and Chen Yun. It should be noted that Chen Yun and Kang Sheng worked under the leadership of Zhou Enlai, Wang Ming and Qin Bangxian long before they met Mao Zedong.

Qin Bangxian, Zhang Wentian and Lu Futan formed the Standing Committee (Li Zhiying 1994: 96). Zhou Enlai was still in Shanghai, but planned his departure for the Jiangxi Soviet, which was repeatedly delayed.

In the following chapters Qin Bangxian will be called 'general secretary'; he was never elected according to the Party statutes, but in the following years he was the highest ranking CCP leader and acknowledged by the Comintern. Strictly speaking, from Xiang Zhongfa's death in 1931 to the 1950s, the Communist Party had no general secretary.

Table 12: The provisional Party leadership from September 1931

Status until September	Names
Politburo member	Lu Futan
Politburo alternate member	–
Central Committee member	–
Central Committee alternate member	Chen Yun
Other	**Qin Bangxian, Zhang Wentian, Li Zhusheng**, Kang Sheng

['28 Bolsheviks' = **bold**]'
(Source: Liu Jintian 1992: 3)

SUMMARY

A careful analysis of the Fourth Plenum shows that a sudden 'takeover' of the CCP leadership by the '28 Bolsheviks' in January 1931 did not take place. Only a few 'Bolsheviks' attended and very few entered the Central Committee and Politburo. Moreover, there is no reliable evidence for the promotion of Wang Ming to the post of general secretary in the following summer. As Li Lisan had left China one month before the plenum and as Xiang Zhongfa and Zhou Enlai managed to adjust to the new line and remain in the leadership, the main effect of the Plenum was not the eradication of the 'leftist Li Lisan group', but in connection with the execution of He Mengxiong and expulsion of Luo Zhanglong, the suppression of the 'rightists'.

The relatively strong position of the 'Bolsheviks' at the end of 1931 was the result of numerous unpredictable developments. Several Central Committee members left Shanghai for the Soviet districts; others, including general secretary Xiang Zhongfa, were arrested and executed. Several leading communists were expelled from the leadership and/or the CCP. In the autumn of 1931, when Wang Ming returned to Moscow and Zhou Enlai moved to Jiangxi, Lu Futan was the only Politburo member re-maining in Shanghai.

47

The development of the CCP leadership in 1931 shows that Zhou Enlai played a decisive role. Wang Ming and Qin Bangxian both relied on Zhou's experience in organisational and security matters and without his support they probably would not have survived the arrests of general secretary Xiang Zhongfa and security chief Gu Shunzhang. In 1931, two other communists with close links to Wang Ming also joined the Party leadership: Chen Yun and Kang Sheng. After Zhou Enlai's departure they were the most important supporters of Qin Bangxian and remained in the leadership for more than four decades.

THREE

The Transfer of CCP Leaders to Jiangxi and Struggle for Power in the Soviet Area (1931–1934)

For many decades, Western accounts of CCP history emphasised the conflict between Mao Zedong and the '28 Bolsheviks' and followed the interpretation given in the Central Committee *Resolution on some Questions in the History of Our Party,* which said:

> Comrades upholding the correct line, with Comrade Mao Tse-tung [Mao Zedong] as their representative, totally opposed the third 'left' line during the period of its dominance. Since they disapproved of it and demanded its rectification, their correct leadership in various districts was removed by the Central Committee reconstituted at the plenary session of January 1931. (Central Committee 1953: 187)

One of many examples for this argument can be found in an article by Henry Schwarz:

> The Kiangsi period's chief importance was the acute struggle for supremacy in the Party between the group around Mao Tse-tung, Chu Te [Zhu De], and other leaders in the Central Soviet Area and the so-called Twenty-eight Bolsheviks. (Schwarz 1970: 547)

In the late 1980s this argument was still very common:

> It will be well known that the political leadership of the time consisted mainly of two groupings – the Maoists on the one hand and the so-called 'Twenty-eight Bolsheviks' group and their followers on the other. (Lötveit 1987: 149)

Many Western authors have argued that many or most of the 'Bolsheviks' went to the Soviet area and gained control of the leadership. John Rue claimed:

> Po Ku [Qin Bangxian], Chang Wen-t'ien [Zhang Wentian], Wang Chia-hsiang [Wang Jiaxiang], and Chou En-lai [Zhou Enlai] arrived in the late summer or early autumn [1931] (Rue 1966: 246)

Robert North suggested another date:

> During the autumn of 1932, Wang Ming, Chang Wen-t'ien [Zhang Wentian], Po Ku [Qin Bangxian), Shen Tse-min [Shen Zemin], and other Central Committeemen moved to Juichin. Shortly thereafter Wang Ming was relieved as secretary-general and was recalled to the Soviet Union. (North 1972: 4)

Stuart Schram (and other scholars) emphasised the connection between the transfer of the '28 Bolsheviks' and the weakening of Mao's position:

> The Twenty-Eight Bolsheviks, having taken control of the party in early 1931, then proceeded in the summer and autumn of 1931 to come to the base area. Progressively, Mao was pushed more and more to one side. (Schram 1983: 23)

Immanuel Hsü provided the following description:

> The Twenty-Eight Bolsheviks [...] arrived in Mao's capital, not with the intention of supporting his movement but of chastising his unorthodox conduct. [...] The Twenty-Eight Bolsheviks rejected the Maoist approach and intended to replace his machine. (Hsü 1995: 556)

These examples show that the importance of the transfer of the '28' has always been emphasised, but that there has been great confusion concerning exact names and dates.

A close look at the biographies of the '28' indicates that only a minority went to Jiangxi. Among the CCP leaders who entered Jiangxi (see Table 13) these few 'Bolsheviks' also represented a minority (Chen Xianqiang 1985: 56ff.). The above-mentioned large number of arrests in Shanghai indicates that many 'Bolsheviks' went into prison, before they could leave the city. Other 'Bolsheviks', such as Chen Changhao, Shen Zemin, Xia Xi and Zhang Qinqiu (see above), went to other communist base areas. Wang Ming and

Table 13: Arrival of leading CCP members in the Jiangxi Soviet (1931–33)

Name	Time
Xiang Ying (PBM)	January 1931
Ren Bishi (PBM), Gu Zuolin, **Wang Jiaxiang**	April 1931
Deng Fa (CCM)	July 1931
Zhou Enlai (PBM)	December 1931
Wang Shengrong	1931
Liu Shaoqi	end of 1932
Qin Bangxian, Chen Yun, **Zhang Wentian, Yang Shangkun**	January 1933
He Kequan, Li Weihan	April 1933

Note: '28 Bolsheviks' = **bold**
(Sources: see main text)

Meng Qingshu never entered the Soviet but returned to Moscow in the autumn of 1931 (see above). In fact, only six or seven of the '28' reached the Central Soviet. Wang Jiaxiang arrived in the spring of 1931, Wang Shengrong followed in the same year (Wang Jiaxiang xuanji bianjizu 1985: 232); until the end of 1932 they were the only 'Bolsheviks' in Jiangxi. Only in early 1933 did the Central Committee leaders Qin Bangxian, Zhang Wentian and Yang Shangkun enter the Soviet area (Li Zhiying 1994: 103; Cheng Zhongyuan 1993: 151). He Kequan arrived in April 1933 (Yi Shaolin 1994: 171).

XIANG YING AND THE ESTABLISHMENT OF THE CENTRAL BUREAU IN JIANGXI

For a long time, the establishment of the Central Bureau in Jiangxi has been linked to the Fourth Plenum of 7 January 1931. 'At any rate, Hsiang Ying was assigned to the post of secretary of the central bureau for the soviet area after the Fourth Plenum' (Kim 1973: 61).

Even in fairly recent publications this view is quite common as the following quote from Benjamin Yang shows: 'At the suggestion of Pavel Mif at the Fourth Plenum, the Central Soviet Bureau was formed in January 1931' (Yang 1990: 49).

Hu Chi-hsi is even more precise:

> On January 15, 1931, two days after the end of the 4th plenum, (*sic!*) the Central Committee announced that a Central Bureau was to be set up in the Jiangxi Soviet and was to assume control of all party organizations in the Soviet areas, including its Red Army sections. To carry out this decision, the Central Committee sent out representatives faithful to the line of the new Politburo into each of the three main Soviet areas [...] Xiang Ying, followed by Zhou Enlai, to the Jiangxi Soviet. (Hu 1988: 159f.)

These and many other authors underestimated the speed of the political changes and overestimated the speed of travelling at that time. The creation of the Central Bureau had already been announced in a Central Committee document of 29 August 1930 when Li Lisan was still dominating the leadership. Guan Xiangying had been named secretary and Zhu De, Mao Zedong, Peng Dehuai, Yuan Guoping, Shi Wenbin and Wang Shoudao were to be members. But Guan Xiangying did not reach the Soviet area (Liao Gailong 1991: 252).

On 3 October 1930 the Politburo in Shanghai reconfirmed its decision to establish a Central Bureau in the Central Soviet. Two weeks later, on 17 October, a decision on its membership was made: Zhou Enlai, Mao Zedong, Xiang Ying, Ren Bishi, Zhu De, Wu Zhenpeng, Yu Fei and two other persons. Zhou Enlai was appointed secretary of the Bureau, Xiang Ying was to be acting secretary until Zhou's arrival in the Soviet. This decision was made before Li Lisan was overthrown; at that time, the '28 Bolsheviks' did not exert any influence on Party policy; the list of Central Bureau members did not include any 'Bolshevik'. In late December 1930 the CC representative Xiang Ying arrived in the Central Soviet (Li Liangming 1993: 72).

On 15 January 1931 the Central Bureau was established in Xiaobu (Ningdu county) and Xiang Ying was the acting secretary. Other members were Zhou Enlai, Ren Bishi, Mao Zedong, Zhu De, Yu Fei, Zeng Shan and two other persons. At the same time, a new Central military commission was established. Xiang Ying became chairman,

Zhu De and Mao Zedong his deputies. Xiang Ying who was neither close to the '28 Bolsheviks' nor to Mao Zedong thus gained a dominant position in a very short time (Guo Zhiming 1987: 3).

The new Central Bureau was, however, unable to function as planned. Zhou Enlai, Ren Bishi and Yu Fei had not yet arrived; Mao Zedong and Zhu De were with the Red Army and could not participate in the Central Bureau's work. As there was no radio communication with Shanghai, the Party Central was not able to control the Soviet or transmit instructions. Even though the Central Bureau first met after the Fourth Plenum, Xiang Ying could only inform the Bureau about the Third Plenum of September 1930 (Zhengzhi xueyuan zhonggong dangshi jiaoyanshi 1985: 137). Thus, the establishment of the Central Bureau had little direct consequences.

THE ARRIVAL OF REN BISHI AND WANG JIAXIANG IN THE SOVIET AREA

After the Fourth Plenum, there was no particular haste in propagating the new line in the Soviet districts. A whole month passed before the Politburo decided – on 6 February – that Xiang Ying, Ren Bishi, Mao Zedong and Wang Jiaxiang should form the Central Bureau's standing committee; on 13 February a more detailed plan was passed. In the following month, on 4 March, it was decided that Ren Bishi, Wang Jiaxiang and Gu Zuolin should travel from Shanghai to the Jiangxi Soviet (Zhonggong zhongyang wenxian yanjiushi 1993: 163–165).

Thus, it took more than three months until the changes in leadership and policy decided at the Fourth Plenum started to affect the Soviet. The delegation sent by the Politburo (Ren Bishi, Gu Zuolin and Wang Jiaxiang) reached the Jiangxi Soviet in the middle of April. Wang Jiaxiang was the first of the '28 Bolsheviks' who entered the Jiangxi Soviet. But as we have seen above, he was neither a Politburo nor Central Committee member and very few communists in Jiangxi had heard his name. In contrast, Ren Bishi, the head of the delegation had joined the CCP in 1922, entered the CC in 1927 and had been promoted to the Politburo in January 1931; he had studied in Moscow long before the 'Bolsheviks' did and was well-known and influential (Zhonggong zhongyang wenxian yanjiushi 1993: 23ff.).

Figure 4: The Central Bureau in Jiangxi in November 1931 (*from left to right*): Gu Zuolin, Ren Bishi, Zhu De, Deng Fa, Xiang Ying, Mao Zedong and Wang Jiaxiang, the only 'Bolshevik'.

On 17 April, the first meeting of the members of the Central Bureau with Ren Bishi, Gu Zuolin and Wang Jiaxiang was held in Qingtang near Ningdu. More than three months after the Fourth Plenum, its decisions were now announced in the Soviet. To improve the efficiency of the Central Bureau, five new members were added; it is, however, not known if the Party leadership in Shanghai accepted this decision. (Guo Zhiming 1987: 3).

After the arrival of the delegation from Shanghai there were differing views within the Central Bureau concerning the military activities, particularly in the Donggu area. Following consultations with several commanders and political commissars the members of the delegation approved of Mao Zedong's and Zhu De's strategy. (Wang Jin 1992: 1143; Zhonggong zhongyang wenxian yanjiushi 1993: 167)

In this context, a speech by Mao Zedong at the Seventh Party congress of 1945 is very interesting. Mao advocated Wang Jiaxiang's election to the Central Committee and emphasised Wang Jiaxiang's and Ren Bishi's contributions after their arrival in the Soviet area (Mao Zedong 1945: 32–33).

In October 1966, Mao Zedong made another favourable comment on Wang Jiaxiang. After criticising Zhang Wentian and Wang Ming, he continued: 'I have a favourable impression of Wang Chia-hsiang, for he approved of the battle at Tungku [Donggu]' (Mao 1966: 268). This was the only reference concerning Wang in a speech that only briefly covered the 1930s; it demonstrates that Mao was grateful for Wang's support and remembered the event for decades.

One possible reason for the lack of a serious conflict between Mao Zedong and the Central delegation was the fact that there were much more serious contradictions between the delegation and Xiang Ying. It has already been mentioned that Xiang Ying had been sent to Jiangxi to push through policies decided at the Third Plenum. In addition, Xiang Ying was closer to the already dismissed Li Lisan and general secretary Xiang Zhongfa than to the '28 Bolsheviks'. After the arrival of the delegation, Xiang Ying was blamed for the mishandling of the investigation into the Futian Incident of December 1930. With Xiang Zhongfa's arrest and execution in June 1931, Xiang Ying lost his most important ally (Liu Mianyu 1991: 202–204). This suggests that in the first half of 1931 there was no serious conflict between Mao and the first 'Bolshevik' in the Soviet, Wang Jiaxiang. In comparison with the Politburo members Xiang Ying and Ren Bishi, Wang Jiaxiang played a minor role.

THE FIRST CONGRESS OF THE JIANGXI SOVIET

After the arrival of the CC delegation Mao's position seems to have been relatively strong, Xiang Ying's position rather weak: in May 1931 Mao was made acting secretary of the Central Bureau (Wang Jin 1992: 58).

On 23 May the First Army established a new front committee and Mao Zedong also headed this. (Wang Jin 1992: 1143; Pang 1993: 344) Until November, Mao was in a strong position.

Following repeated announcements and delays, the first congress of the Chinese Soviet opened in Ruijin in November 1931 and a provisional government was established. The congress began on 7 November, the anniversary of the Russian October revolution, and ended on 20 November. The election of a government was intended to demonstrate the strength of the communist movement. Therefore, great efforts were made to publicise draft laws, resolutions and election results in the whole of China (*Fundamental Laws of the Chinese Soviet Republic*, 1934; Hinz 1973: 466ff.).

Still, for many decades, many aspects related to the congress remained in the dark. This included the identity of prominent participants. Derek Waller, who has studied the Soviet congress in detail, argues that many 'Bolsheviks' went to Jiangxi and draws far-reaching conclusions concerning the relationship between the communist government and the Party:

> But despite the fact that many of the Returned Students moved from the headquarters in Shanghai to Juichin [Ruijin] so as to attend the Congress, Mao and his supporters, because of their entrenched influence in the soviet administrative and electoral machinery, won control of the government created by the Congress. The Returned Students, however, clearly won command of the Party apparatus in the Central Soviet Area. (Waller 1973: 112)

Rue described the arrival and departure of several CCP leaders:

> Po Ku [Qin Bangxian] and Chang Wen-t'ien [Zhang Wentian], who were there, were not elected to anything. [...]
>
> Delegates from other soviet areas left for their home bases, and

Po Ku, Chang Wen-t'ien, and most of the other Politburo members left for Shanghai. Mao, Hsiang Ying [Xiang Ying] and Chou En-lai [Zhou Enlai] remained in the new soviet capital Jui-ching [Ruijin]. (Rue 1966: 246ff.)

A similar account was provided by Immanuel Hsü:

After the Congress, Po Ku [Qin Bangxian] and most of the other Politburo members returned to Shanghai, in preparation for the next round of dueling with Mao. (Hsü 1995: 557)

The biographical sources currently available do not confirm these claims. Qin Bangxian, Zhang Wentian and other prominent communists in Shanghai did not travel to Jiangxi to participate in the congress. The journey was long, difficult and – for communists – extremely dangerous. The same was true for senior leaders of the other communist bases: Zhang Guotao and Shen Zemin also failed to attend. Zhou Enlai only arrived in December – after the end of the congress.

Here are some important results of the Soviet congress:

On 25 November, the Central Revolutionary Military committee was established and included fifteen members: Zhu De, Peng Dehuai, Wang Jiaxiang, Lin Biao, Tan Zhenlin, Ye Jianying, Kong Hechong, Zhou Enlai, Zhang Guotao, Shao Shiping, He Long, Mao Zedong, Xu Xiangqian, Guan Xiangying and Wang Shengrong. Zhou Enlai, Zhang Guotao and some other members were not in the Central Soviet. Only two 'Bolsheviks', Wang Jiaxiang and Wang Shengrong, were included. Zhu De became chairman, Wang Jiaxiang and Peng Dehuai his deputies. These three leaders may have disagreed with Mao Zedong in a number of questions, but they were not his enemies or opponents. It can be assumed that Mao was supported by the majority of the committee members who were in Jiangxi in November 1931 (Liao Gailong 1991: 269–70).

On 27 November Mao Zedong was appointed chairman of the Central Executive Committee, with Xiang Ying and Zhang Guotao (absent) as deputies. On the same day Mao became chairman of the Council of People's Commissars. People's Commissars (Ministers) were Zhu De (Military Affairs), Xiang Ying (Labour), Deng Zihui (Finance), Zhang Dingcheng (Land), Qu Qiubai (Education), Zhou Yili (Internal Affairs), Zhang Guotao (Law), He Shuheng (Inspection) and – the only 'Bolshevik' – Wang Jiaxiang (Foreign Affairs) (Zhengzhi xueyuan zhonggong dangshi jiaoyanshi 1985: 144–145).

Many appointments only had a symbolic meaning as some prominent persons chosen (Zhang Guotao, Qu Qiubai) were not in the Soviet area; Wang Jiaxiang, the only 'Bolshevik' appointed, became people's commissar for foreign affairs, when there were hardly any foreign affairs.

All in all, in November 1931, Mao Zedong's position in the Soviet area was quite strong and the '28 Bolsheviks' did not have much influence.

THE ARRIVAL OF ZHOU ENLAI AND MAO ZEDONG'S DEMOTION

Zhou Enlai reached the Central Soviet in late December 1931 – several weeks after the end of the first Soviet congress. In Autumn 1930, Zhou had been appointed secretary of the Central Bureau. With Zhou's arrival Mao Zedong's role as acting secretary ended (Pang Xianzhi 1993: 363–364). On 7 January 1932, Zhou Enlai took over the leadership of the Central Bureau (Li Ping 1989: 215–216).

At that time, a controversy concerning an attack on the city of Ganzhou erupted. Mao opposed the plan, arguing that the enemy was too strong. The Central Bureau, however, supported the idea and started preparations for the attack. At the end of January, the Central Bureau relieved Mao of his duties 'for health reasons' (Pang Xianzhi 1993: 364–366).

In his article *Problems of Strategy in China's Revolutionary War* of 1936, Mao Zedong argued:

> By May 1928 basic principles of guerilla warfare, simple in nature and suited to the conditions of the time, had already been evolved. [...] But beginning from January 1932 [...] the 'Left' opportunists attacked these correct principles. [...] From then on, the old principles were no longer to be considered as regular but were to be rejected as 'guerilla-ism'. The opposition to 'guerrila-ism' reigned for three whole years. (Mao 1936: 213–214)

Following the arrival of Zhou Enlai, Mao Zedong lost power. Zhou was not only a representative of the Central leadership in Shanghai, but one of the most senior Chinese communists and the only

Figure 5: Zhou Enlai (*with beard*) in Jiangxi in 1933.

member of the Politburo's standing committee in Jiangxi. Zhou was also head of the CC Military commission and – in contrast to Xiang Ying, Ren Bishi and Wang Jiaxiang – gained considerable military experience during the Northern Expedition. Zhou therefore also knew many military leaders in the Soviet.

In 1941, at the beginning of the Rectification Movement, Mao criticised CCP politics of the early 1930s and described 1932 (when Zhou Enlai took over command in the Soviet) as the first year of the wrong line (Mao Zedong 1941: 2). This date is not relevant in connection with Wang Ming, Qin Bangxian and other 'Bolsheviks'. During four years of discussions which led to the passing of the *Resolution on some questions in the history of Our Party* (1945), January 1931 (Fourth Plenum) and September 1931 (reorganisation of the leadership) gained importance as they could be linked to the rise of Wang Ming and Qin Bangxian. In the published version of the *Resolution,* which was a compromise paper intended to unify the majority of CCP leaders, these two politicians were explicitly criticised but Zhou Enlai was not mentioned. For Mao, who in 1931 was not in Shanghai and who was not directly affected by the changes there, Zhou Enlai's arrival in Jiangxi was far more important.

In March 1932, after the failure of the attack on Ganzhou, Xiang Ying went to Mao and asked him to return and participate in military planning. (Pang Xianzhi 1993: 367) Mao's knowledge and experience were again considered useful. In the following six months Mao took part in several military campaigns, which were led by Zhou Enlai.

In the autumn a sharp controversy arose at the Ningdu Conference. This conference is one of the most problematic in most accounts of CCP history. The first problem is the date, which has been discussed for decades. The identification of the participants and the evaluation of its decisions was also very difficult. In China there has been an obvious hesitance in dealing with this controversial subject, and Zhou Enlai's role was the main problem.

Hu Chi-hsi, an expert in Chinese military affairs living in France, published the following description:

> The Ningdu conference was held, in all likelihood, during the very first days of August since, on August 8, the Revolutionary Military Council published a directive to the Red Army at Xingguo, announcing the tasks to be accomplished for the fourth campaign, which had undoubtedly been decided upon at this meeting. (Hu 1988: 172–3)

August has also been suggested by many other scholars as the most likely date, but recent Chinese sources show that the Ningdu Conference only happened in October 1932 (Li Ping 1989: 231; Pang Xianzhi 1993: 389–390). The conference was a meeting of the Central Bureau with eight members attending, the secretary of the Central Bureau, Zhou Enlai, chaired the conference. Four of the participants (Ren Bishi, Xiang Ying, Gu Zuolin and Deng Fa) came from Ruijin, the other four (Zhou Enlai, Mao Zedong, Zhu De and Wang Jiaxiang) belonged to the front committee (Li Ping 1989: 231; Pang Xianzhi 1993: 1/389–390).

It is also known that the discussions concentrated on military strategy and that Mao's views were not supported by the majority. The most important result was the immediate granting of 'sick leave' to Mao, which had been suggested by Zhou Enlai. Mao thus left the front committee and was for the next two years (until the beginning of the Long March) not involved in military affairs. On 26 October 1932, Zhou Enlai was officially appointed successor of Mao as political commissar of the First Front Army (Li Ping 1989: 231–233; Pang Xianzhi 1993: 1/389–390). On 8 May 1933, Zhou's position was further strengthened by his additional appointment as political commissar of the whole Red Army (Li Ping 1989: 245–246).

Even though detailed and reliable sources are not available, there are many indications that Zhou Enlai was responsible for Mao's dismissal. It is very unlikely that the highest ranking CCP member present, Zhou Enlai, who was also secretary of the Central Bureau and chairman of the military commission, would have been outvoted in military matters by other members not involved in these. There are also a number of sources indicating that Mao received support from Zhu De and Wang Jiaxiang, the only 'Bolshevik' present. If Zhou had also supported Mao, there could not have been a majority against Mao. (Jiang Huaxuan 1991: 133; Pang Xianzhi 1993: 1/389–390)

There is no doubt that Mao was deprived of power after Zhou Enlai's arrival in the Soviet and before the arrival of the Central leadership in the following year. The 'Bolsheviks' did not play an important role in this.

THE ARRIVAL OF THE PROVISIONAL CCP LEADERSHIP AND THE CAMPAIGN AGAINST THE 'LUO MING LINE'

Following the numerous arrests of CCP leaders in 1931 and 1932 and the transfer of Wang Ming and Kang Sheng to Moscow, the remaining members of the Party leadership decided in late 1932 to leave Shanghai and move to the Central Soviet. Still, after the departure of Kang Sheng and arrest of Lu Futan, the important transfer of the provisional Party Centre to Jiangxi involved only three persons.

In January 1933, Qin Bangxian, Zhang Wentian and Chen Yun arrived in Jiangxi. For the first time the CCP leadership now resided in the Party's most important base area. According to currently available sources there was no immediate conflict between the newcomers and Mao Zedong. In the first few months there was no major conference or Plenum. After the arrival of the Shanghai leaders, the provisional leadership and the Central Bureau of the Soviet were combined. Mao Zedong thus became a full member of the Politburo and improved his formal position (Li Ping 1989: 241; Li Zhiying 1994: 103; Cheng Zhongyuan 1993: 151; Wang Jin 1992: 1307).

Concerning the motives for the move to Jiangxi, Otto Braun provided an interesting detail which cannot be found in or verified by Chinese accounts:

> There was later the additional consideration that the Central Soviet Area's political administration would be substantially strengthened and that the tension felt between Chou En-lai [Zhou Enlai] and Mao Tse-tung [Mao Zedong] since the Ningtu [Ningdu] Conference might be reduced. (Braun 1982: 25)

In February 1933, a campaign against the 'opportunistic Luo Ming line' started in Fujian and soon included the fight against the 'Luo Ming line in Jiangxi'. The main representatives of the 'incorrect' line were said to be Luo Ming, Mao Zedong's brother Mao Zetan, Deng Xiaoping, Xie Weijun and Gu Bo, as well as Deng Zihui and Xiao Jinguang. They and dozens of other communists were criticised and dismissed (Luo Ming 1982: 234ff.; Lü Cheng 1992: 92).

This campaign was hardly mentioned in early Western studies (Schwartz 1951; Compton 1952; Brandt et al. 1952). Only after its appearance in the *Resolution on some questions in the history of our Party* did it become more prominent and was used to emphasise the confrontation between Mao and the 'Bolsheviks' (Swarup 1966: 250ff.; Guillermaz 1972: 222–223; Yang 1990: 72).

But it was rarely noticed that – apart from Qin Bangxian – Li Weihan, Gu Zuolin, Ren Bishi and Zhou Enlai were very active in this campaign, which therefore should not be described as a campaign of the '28 Bolsheviks' against Mao (Li Weihan 1986: 335–337).

In the PRC this campaign was treated in a mysterious way: on the one hand, since the *Resolution on some questions in the history of Our Party*, it has been repeatedly described as 'wrong', 'leftist' and 'anti-Mao' on the other hand, for many decades no detailed account of the campaign appeared. In the 1980s some surviving activists (Li Weihan 1986) and victims (Luo Ming 1982) finally commented on it. Li Weihan at least admitted in his memoirs that he wrongly attacked Deng Xiaoping, Mao Zetan and others (Li Weihan 1986: 335–337); but even in the late 1980s Zhou Enlai's activities and publications in this campaign were not revealed. When political events of this period are discussed, the role of Zhou Enlai still seems to be the main problem and his name is usually not mentioned.

THE FIFTH PLENUM AND THE LOSS OF JIANGXI

The Fifth Plenum of the Sixth Central Committee belongs to the least studied and documented plenary sessions of the CC. According to the *Resolution on some questions in the history of Our Party*, this plenum 'marked the height of the third "left" line' (Central Committee 1953: 186). Still, for many decades, no detailed account of this negative event was published in China. Outside China, there are hardly any relevant sources.

This plenum was very important as it was the first after the execution of the last general secretary Xiang Zhongfa, the unusual promotion of Qin Bangxian and the transfer of the Central leadership to Jiangxi in 1933.

The number and identity of participants has never been published. As a Politburo member, Mao belonged to the potential participants, but his appearance has often been doubted. Otto Braun, who arrived in the Soviet in the autumn of 1933, provided interesting background information, which does not appear in other sources:

> Even before the Central Committee Plenum he [Mao] introduced a note of discord into the apparent harmony by stating that his poor health would not permit his participation. He actually did stay away. Po Ku [Qin Bangxian] remarked sarcastically that Mao was once again suffering from a 'diplomatic disorder' because he was offended that Lo Fu [Zhang Wentian] rather than he was to give the report 'On the Chinese Soviet Movement and its tasks' and that his demand to be admitted into the Politburo's Standing Committee had not been granted. (Braun 1982: 49)

Braun probably exaggerated the 'apparent harmony', but recent Chinese sources confirm Mao Zedong's absence. (Pang Xianzhi 1993: 1/420)

The three main reports of the Plenum were presented by Qin Bangxian (on the CCP), Zhang Wentian (on the government) and Chen Yun (on the KMT-ruled 'White areas'), several resolutions were passed. There is no reliable information about other reports and the contents of the discussions (Lü Cheng 1991: 97).

At the Fifth Plenum the 'Bolsheviks' Wang Jiaxiang and He Kequan finally became members of the CC, Yang Shangkun alternate member (Liu Jintian 1992: 3).

More important was the establishment of a new Secretariat, which functioned as a Standing Committee of the Politburo. Following telegraphic consultations with the Comintern in Moscow in December 1933, Qin Bangxian, Zhou Enlai, Zhang Wentian, Chen Yun, Wang Ming and Zhang Guotao were promoted to the Secretariat. Wang Ming and Zhang Guotao, who were not in the Jiangxi Soviet, were suggested by the Comintern. Their inclusion had no immediate consequences, but was important during and after the Long March (Li Yunlong 1987: 14–15). Thus the top of the Party in the Soviet consisted of Qin Bangxian, Zhang Wentian, Zhou Enlai and Chen Yun. All four were born in Shanghai or Jiangsu and had arrived in Jiangxi between December 1931 and January 1933. Mao Zedong, who remained in the Politburo, and other communists of the old Soviet were not represented in the Secretariat.

Only three months after the political reorganisation of January 1934 the Red Army lost an important battle at Guangchang. The military situation worsened and preparations for leaving the Central Soviet began. In October 1934 – two years after Mao's dismissal at the Ningdu Conference – the Long March started.

SUMMARY

For several decades numerous authors claimed that most or all 'Bolsheviks' went to the Jiangxi Soviet and clashed with Mao Zedong. The biographies of the '28 Bolsheviks' do, however, show that only half a dozen of them reached Jiangxi. Many important 'Bolsheviks', including Wang Ming, Shen Zemin, Chen Changhao, Xia Xi and Sheng Zhongliang never went to Jiangxi. In 1931 and 1932 just two 'Bolsheviks' entered Jiangxi, only in 1933 they were joined by four others, including Qin Bangxian and Zhang Wentian. By that time, Mao Zedong had already lost most of his influence. The people responsible for weakening Mao's position were not 'Bolsheviks', but other CCP leaders including Xiang Ying, Ren Bishi, Gu Zuolin, Deng Fa and in particular Zhou Enlai. With respect to his formal position in the Party hierarchy, Mao, in fact, benefited from the arrival of the Shanghai leaders in 1933: when the Shanghai and Jiangxi leaderships were amalgamated, he became a member of the Politburo. At the Fifth Plenum in January 1934, he was again elected to the Politburo, but did not enter its Secretariat. Between 1932 and 1934 Mao had little influence in political and military affairs. In several campaigns, such as the struggle against the 'Luo Ming line', his supporters were also attacked. As the strategies of the new leadership failed and the Soviet area was lost in 1934, Mao ultimately profited from not having been a member of the top leadership. Unlike Zhou Enlai, Qin Bangxian and Otto Braun, Mao could not be blamed for the failures and losses of the preceding years.

FOUR

Struggles within the CCP Leadership during the Long March

In this chapter several important events concerning changes in the Party leadership during the Long March and, particularly, the Zunyi Conference of January 1935 will be analysed. In China and in Western countries, the Long March is often described as the most important event in the development of the Communist Party and the rise of Mao Zedong. The Zunyi Conference is seen as 'one of the most important conferences in the history of the CCP and of the Chinese Revolution' (Kim 1992: 435), as the turning-point during the March, as the end of defeats and losses of the Red Army and the beginning of the 'liberation' of China, and also as the end of 'incorrect' 'Leftist' policies and the beginning of the 'correct' leadership by Mao Zedong. In one of his last books, John K. Fairbank stated: 'Mao regained the leadership of the CCP in early 1935 and thereafter never relinquished it.' (Fairbank 1986: 234).

This view is based on Hu Qiaomu's publication of 1951, the *Resolution on some Questions in the History of Our Party* (Central Committee 1953) and was confirmed by the 1981 *Resolution on CCP history since 1949.*

> In January 1935, the Political Bureau of the Central Committee of the Party convened a meeting in Zunyi during the Long March, which established the leading position of Comrade Mao Zedong in the Red Army and the Central Committee of the Party. This saved the Red Army and the Central Committee of the Party which were then in critical danger and subsequently made it possible to [...] bring the Long March to a triumphant

conclusion and open up new vistas for the Chinese Revolution. It was a vital turning point in the history of the Party. (*Resolution* 1981: 6)

On the following pages the appropriateness of these statements will be analysed.

THE BEGINNING OF THE LONG MARCH AND THE CONFERENCES IN DECEMBER 1934

In the autumn of 1934 the Red Army was no longer able to defend the Central Soviet and fled from Jiangxi – this campaign later became famous as the Long March. Originally, the March was supposed to go to neighbouring Hunan province and was not planned to be long. But as KMT and warlord troops blocked the planned route and attacked the communists, the Red Army moved further to the West and suffered great losses. Due to these losses and the frustration of soldiers and commanders, who did not understand the purpose of the campaign, there were numerous discussions concerning the future (Nie 1988: 199ff.).

For many decades Chinese and foreign scholars have concentrated their research on the 'historical' Zunyi Conference, but ignored important conferences in the weeks before the arrival in Zunyi. The meetings in Tongdao, Liping and Houchang were hardly known. It is now known, that some important controversies and decisions long associated with the Zunyi Conference of January 1935 happened earlier and that the balance of power had already changed in December 1934 (see Kampen 1986: 349–350; Kampen 1989b: 708–709).

The reasons behind these consultations were the above-mentioned heavy losses of the Red Army in the first two months of the Long March. The number of soldiers dropped from 90,000 in October to 30,000 in early December. One reason for these losses was the attempt by Qin Bangxian, Zhou Enlai and Otto Braun, to move northwards, where strong enemy troops blocked the way and attacked the Red Army (Liao Gailong 1991: 301–302).

Otto Braun described these developments in his memoirs:

In order to avoid enemy flank assaults and natural barriers the 1st Corps was forced to turn back and link up with the central column. Almost a week was lost by this, permitting strong

Kwangtung and Central Kuomintang forces to pursue and engage the 5th and 9th Corps in days of bloody rearguard battles. This incident was immediately exploited by Mao Tse-tung, Lo Fu [Zhang Wentian] and Wang Chia-hsiang in a vigorous attack against Po Ku [Qin Bangxian], Chou En-lai [Zhou Enlai], and, above all me. We conceded that a mistake was made in determining the 1st Corps' route, but it was not, as Chou En-lai expressed it, 'of a systematic nature'. What was to blame was faulty intelligence. (Braun 1982: 88–89)

Braun's description and particularly the emphasis on the support Mao received from two 'Bolsheviks', Wang Jiaxiang and Zhang Wentian, were confirmed by recent Chinese sources. These developments will be discussed below.

On 12 December 1934, Party and Army leaders (including Qin Bangxian, Zhou Enlai, Otto Braun, Mao Zedong, Wang Jiaxiang and Zhang Wentian) met in Tongdao in the south of Hunan to discuss the direction the Army should move. Qin Bangxian and Otto Braun continued to advocate the original plan to move to the North. Mao suggested that troops should march to Guizhou Province in the West to avoid engagements with superior enemy forces. First Wang Jiaxiang, then Zhang Wentian and finally – for the first time in several years – Zhou Enlai supported Mao's plan and it was decided to march to Liping in Guizhou. Thus, two years after the Ningdu Conference, Mao regained influence in military planning (Li Zhiguang 1983: 22; Li Ping 1989: 268; Pang Xianzhi 1993: 1/439; Cheng Zhongyuan 1993: 195–196; Li Zhiying 1994: 166–168).

On 18 December, after the arrival in Liping, the Politburo held its first meeting since the beginning of the Long March. Zhou Enlai chaired the conference, Mao Zedong, Qin Bangxian, Wang Jiaxiang, Zhang Wentian and others took part. Mao suggested that the original plan of joining the Second and Sixth Armies should be abandoned; instead, a new base area should be established in Northern Guizhou. Qin Bangxian opposed this idea but received no support. Otto Braun is said to have been absent due to bad health; after the Liping conference, he had no impact on the military strategy. The majority supported Mao, and decided to convene a larger meeting in Zunyi to discuss future developments (Li Zhiguang 1983: 22; Li Ping 1989: 269; Pang Xianzhi 1993: 1/440; Cheng Zhongyuan 1993: 196; Li Zhiying 1994: 169–170).

On the night between 31 December and 1 January 1935 the Politburo met in Houchang in Northern Guizhou. It decided to establish a new base in the Sichuan–Guizhou border region and move to the nearest city – Zunyi – to convene an enlarged Politburo meeting. It also decided that important strategical decisions of the military commission had to be submitted to the Politburo for approval. This decision weakened Zhou Enlai and Otto Braun, and, indirectly, included Mao in military planning. (Li Zhiguang 1983: 22–23; Li Ping 1989: 271; Pang Xianzhi 1993: 1/442; Cheng Zhongyuan 1993: 197; Li Zhiying 1994: 170–171)

These developments show that, during December 1934, Mao gradually strengthened his position, while Otto Braun and Qin Bangxian were weakened. The main reason for this development was the disastrous beginning of the Long March for which Zhou, Qin and Braun were responsible. In these conferences Mao Zedong first gained Wang Jiaxiang's support, then the two convinced Zhang Wentian and, finally, Zhou Enlai switched sides and withdrew his support for Qin Bangxian and Otto Braun. Thus the most important changes happened before the opening of the Zunyi Conference.

THE ZUNYI CONFERENCE IN JANUARY 1935

The Zunyi Conference played an important Role in both Chinese and Western history writing and was often characterized as the most important conference, or one of the most important conferences, in the history of the CCP. The following account highlights some important aspects; more details concerning the conference can be found in my earlier publications (Kampen 1986; Kampen 1987; Kampen 1989a; Kampen 1989b).

The former editor of the *China Quarterly*, Dick Wilson, who published one of the first books on the Long March, came to the following conclusion:

> This was the most important Politburo meeting in the Party's entire history, for it dramatically reversed Party policy and reshuffled its leadership in favour of Mao Tse-tung, the man who remained thereafter its dominating personality. (Wilson 1971: 91)

This view is based on Hu Qiaomu's article and the Central Committee *Resolution on some questions in the history of Our Party* which said:

> The broad ranks of cadres and Party members who were opposed to the 'Left' line rallied around Comrade Mao Tse-tung as their leader; and this made it possible for the enlarged meeting of the Central Political Bureau [...] in January 1935 under the leadership of Comrade Mao Tse-tung, to succeed in terminating the rule of the 'Left' line in the Central Committee and in saving the Party at a most critical juncture. [...] The meeting inaugurated a new leadership in the Central Committee with Comrade Mao Tse-tung at the head, and this was a change of paramount historical importance in the Chinese Party. (Central Committee 1953: 188)

This description includes rather vague expressions and lacks a precise description of the 'critical juncture' and the solution of the problems, and there is no exact definition of Mao Zedong's title or position. In the early 1950s this account probably surprised Chinese and Western readers, as no descriptions of the Zunyi Conference had been published between 1935 and 1950. Not even Edgar Snow and Agnes Smedley, who in the late 1930s made detailed interviews with numerous communist leaders, discussed the conference. Thus, the early American publications, written before the appearance of the *Resolution* are very interesting. Schwartz's book, which featured 'The Rise of Mao' in its title, ended with 1933 and Schwartz argued that that year was the time of Mao's 'Victory' and the 'Triumph of Mao Tse-tung' (Schwartz 1951: 172). At about the same time, Compton wrote: 'Mao gained [...] official leadership when he became head of the Politburo in 1937.' (Compton 1952: xxxviii). From 1953 these differences disappeared and the official Chinese date, was accepted all over the world (Brandt 1952: 377; Hsiao 1961: 159; Rue 1966: 352; Ch'en 1967: 189; North 1968: 139; Wilson 1971: 91; Guillermaz 1972: 255; Kim 1973: 3; Dittmar 1975: 101; Donovan 1981: 144; Womack 1982: 173; Bartke 1985: 178; Leung 1992: 509).

Surprisingly, the few vague sentences in the *Resolution* and in Hu Qiaomu's text convinced most foreign scholars; in the 1950s, 1960s and 1970s no detailed descriptions of the conference appeared in China. In the early 1980s the situation suddenly changed, as the Chinese leadership decided to use the fiftieth anniversary of the conference (1985) to propagate the achievements of several rehabilitated CCP leaders. Three participants of the Zunyi Conference – Chen Yun, Deng Xiaoping and Yang Shangkun – were now in the Politburo. These three did not publish detailed accounts, but two other survivors, Nie Rongzhen and Wu Xiuquan, did.

Western scholars had been studying the conference for decades and tried to verify dates, participants and decisions. However, even though they all emphasized the importance of the Zunyi Conference, they did not have sufficient source materials and disagreed on most details.

Date

Concerning the date of the Zunyi Conference many different views were published, including 4 January (Payne 1965: 193), 6–8 January (Kuo 1970: 16; Harrison 1972: 245; Wu 1974: 49; Kuo 1975: 58; Kim 1992: 435), 7–8 January (Braun 1973: 131), 8 January (Kagan 1992: 237) and 15–18 January (Yang 1990: 316). The most common view, that the Conference lasted from 6 to 8 January, was based on the combination of different factors: first, there was a document – often simply called *Resolution of the Zunyi Conference* (see below) – which was dated '8.1.' in its printed versions; second, it was assumed that this document had been passed on the last day of the conference; third, there was widespread agreement that the conference lasted for three days.

It is now known that that document was passed on 8 February and that the date had mistakenly been changed from '8.2.' to '8.1.' when it was first printed (in the early 1940s), as it was assumed that the Zunyi Conference happened in January the date was changed accordingly (see Chapter 6). As this document is the result of another conference (see below), it is not suitable for finding the date of the Zunyi Conference (Li Zhiguang 1983: 16ff.).

In connection with the editing of the *Resolution on Party history* (1981) and the preparations for the fiftieth anniversary of the Zunyi Conference (1985) a group of Beijing Party historians studied numerous CCP documents, army telegrams and memoirs to verify the conference's dates, participants and decisions. Their detailed investigation report shows, that the conference could only have taken place between 15 and 17 January. (Li Zhiguang 1983: 18) Because of the detailed documentation and the fact that earlier attempts to decide on the conference dates were never convincingly documented, this new interpretation has been accepted inside and outside China. Benjamin Yang (see above) also used (a shorter version of) this report, but assumed that there were top-level consultations one day after the big conference (Yang 1990: 110–112); but he could not prove his assumption. His view that '8.1.' was originally '18.1.' is not based on any sources (Yang 1986: 239).

Participants

Western scholars have long disagreed on the number and names of the participants and, particularly, the percentage of CC members, military leaders and other participants. As Braun and other – mainly Soviet – authors (Titov 1976: 102) have argued that elected CC members were outvoted by non-members, this is an important question.

> Mao used the break to force the convening of a so-called 'enlarged' session of the Politburo of the Central Committee. This posed little difficulty because he knew he had most of the Politburo members present in Tsunyi behind him. [...] But that was not enough for him. Members of the Provisional Revolutionary Government, members of General Headquarters, and commanders and commissars of corps and divisions were also invited to the conference which took place on 7–8 January 1935. They formed the great majority, and, contrary to Party regulations and norms, were granted decisive as well as advisory voting powers. Of the thirty-five to forty participants fewer than one-third, probably one-quarter, were members of the Central Committee, not to mention the Politburo. (Braun 1982: 95)

Most of the other scholars suggest a smaller number of participants – Ch'en (1969: 18) 18, Harrison (1972: 245) about 20 and Kuo (1970: 16) over 20.

Most scholars agree on the following participants: Qin Bangxian, Zhang Wentian, Zhou Enlai, Zhu De, Mao Zedong, Peng Dehuai, Liu Bocheng, Lin Biao and Li Fuchun.

Concerning the other participants, views vary considerably.

Ch'en (1969: 18–20) adds Liang Botai and Wu Liangping, doubts the participation of Chen Yun, He Kequan, Wang Jiaxiang and Braun, and claims that Liu Shaoqi did not go on the Long March. According to him Deng Fa, Deng Xiaoping and Teng Daiyuan may have participated.

Kuo (1970:17) adds Chen Yun, Deng Fa, He Kequan, Li Weihan, Liu Shaoqi, Nie Rongzhen, Wang Shoudao and Yang Shangkun, as well as Albert List (=Otto Braun); he argues that Wang Jiaxiang was absent due to his illness.

Harrison (1972: 245) adds Chen Yun, He Kequan, Li Weihan and Liu Shaoqi, as well as Otto Braun.

Chinese sources currently available show that Chen Yun and Liu Shaoqi participated and left the First Army much later (see below); despite his illness, Wang Jiaxiang also took part – all three played a decisive role. He Kequan certainly participated, he was the main supporter of Qin Bangxian. Deng Fa and Nie Rongzhen also took part (Li Zhiguang 1983: 20–21). With the exception of Deng Xiaoping, the other persons mentioned did not take part, as they did not have a leading position in the Party or Army.

Table 14: Participants of the Zunyi Conference (January 1935)

Politburo: members	**Qin Bangxian, Zhang Wentian**, Zhou Enlai, Chen Yun, Zhu De, Mao Zedong
Politburo: alter-nate members	**Wang Jiaxiang, He Kequan**, Liu Shaoqi, Deng Fa
Military	Liu Bocheng, Li Fuchun (CCAM), Lin Biao, Nie Rongzhen, Peng Dehuai (CCAM), **Yang Shangkun** (CCAM), Li Zhuoran,
Comintern	Otto Braun
Other	Deng Xiaoping, Wu Xiuquan

Note: '28 Bolsheviks' = **bold**
(Source: Li Zhiguang 1983: 20–21)

Li Zhiguang's above-mentioned report lists 20 people (see also Table 14), 17 were official participants: six Politburo members, four alternate members of the Politburo, seven Army people, including three CC alternate members; in addition, Otto Braun, his inter-preter Wu Xiuquan, and Deng Xiaoping (as secretary/steno-grapher) took part (Li Zhiguang 1983: 20–21). The total number is not far from Western estimates. If this convincing report is more or less accurate, 13 of the 17 participants were at least alternate members of the CC and 10 at least alternate members of the Politburo. Non-members could not have outvoted CC or Politburo members.

Proceedings

Most of the participants contributed to the discussions, but the order, contents and character of their contributions are not known in detail.

Early Western accounts repeatedly claimed that Mao Zedong was the first speaker, and boldly criticised the leadership. Jerome Ch'en, who used the memoirs of Mao's friend Xiao San as his source, wrote:

> '[...] the first to speak [...] was Mao, who exposed the political and military mistakes committed by the Party Centre. This was followed by Chu Teh's attack on Otto Braun.' (Ch'en 1969: 20)

The currently available sources give another order of speeches: 'general secretary' Qin Bangxian opened the Politburo conference with a general report, and Zhou Enlai followed with a report on the military situation. Then, Zhang Wentian gave a long, critical speech, which was the basis of the later 'resolution' of the Zunyi Conference. Mao Zedong and Wang Jiaxiang supported Zhang's criticism. (Li Zhiguang 1983: 23–24; Li Ping 1989: 272; Pang Xianzhi 1993: 1/443–444; Cheng Zhongyuan 1993: 200ff.; Li Zhiying 1994: 174–175).

Results

Most Western accounts of the Zunyi Conference claim that Mao Zedong became chairman. There has, however, been considerable confusion concerning his precise position.

Kuo (1970: 3/23), Harrison (1972: 246), Wu (1974: 54), Donovan (1981: 144), Domes (1985: 37) and Kim (1992: 435) argued that Mao became chairman of the Military Affairs Committee.

Brandt (1955: 377), Rue (1966: 270), Ch'en (1967: 189; 1969: 36), Selden (1971: 107), Hou (1973: 47) and Bartke (1981: 582) argued that Mao became chairman of the Politburo.

Brandt (1952: 38) claimed, that Mao became chairman of the CC and Politburo. Guillermaz (1972: 255) described Mao as 'temporary Chairman of the Central Committee – in other words, leader of the Communist Party'.

Some scholars not only emphasised changes in the Party leadership, but also in relations to the Comintern.

In the 1930s, the positions of Party, Politburo or Central Committee chairman did, however, not exist. Before and after the conference Zhu De was chairman of the military commission. Zhou Enlai remained political commissar. All the above-mentioned statements are incorrect.

Only the so-called 'Triumvirate' of Qin Bangxian, Zhou Enlai and Otto Braun, which had acted as an unofficial leadership, was dissolved.

Mao was only promoted from a Politburo member to a member of the Secretariat (Pang Xianzhi 1993: 1/443).

Strictly speaking, there was no change at the top of the Party: Qin Bangxian remained 'general secretary'. No 'Bolshevik' or any other person was dismissed from the Politburo or Central Committee.

In January 1935, there was no significant change in the Party leadership.

CHANGES IN THE PARTY AND ARMY LEADERSHIP
AFTER THE ZUNYI CONFERENCE

For a long time changes in the CCP leadership were associated with the Zunyi Conference. It is now known that some important decisions were only made several weeks later (Kampen 1986: 355). On 5 February 1935, Qin Bangxian retired as 'general secretary' and Zhang Wentian took over. Thus, the top position in the Party leadership was given by one 'Bolshevik' to another 'Bolshevik'. Even though the circumstances of this handover are not known in detail, it is obvious that Qin Bangxian managed to hand over the post to the person he knew best and had known for the longest time. This handover cannot be considered as a drastic change or beginning of a new era (Pang 1993: 1/446).

The complicated conflict between the CCP leadership and Zhang Guotao after the meeting of both armies in June 1935 has been treated by many scholars and will not be described here. Zhang Guotao's political and military power was a threat to all other Party leaders, including Mao Zedong (Ch'en 1986: 211ff; Yang 1990: 140ff.). The most important change in the top leadership, which was decided on 18 July 1935, was the handover of the position of political commissar from Zhou Enlai to Zhang Guotao (Li Ping

1989: 285). Mao, who did not have any top leadership position, was not directly affected. The conflict between Zhang Guotao and the other Party leaders was solved through the separation of both armies.

SUMMARY

An analysis of the power struggles within the CCP leadership during the Long March shows that there was no putsch at the Zunyi Conference in January 1935; Mao Zedong did not suddenly take over the leadership of the Party. During six important meetings between December 1934 and March 1935 Mao just gained increasing influence in matters of military planning.

In 1935 leadership posts such as chairman of the Communist Party, chairman of the Central Committee, or chairman of the Politburo did not exist and Mao did not gain any of these titles. We also know that the successor of 'general secretary' Qin Bangxian was Zhang Wentian – another 'Bolshevik'! Mao just entered the Standing Committee of the Politburo. In January 1935 Zhu De remained commander-in-chief and Zhou Enlai was still political commissar. In March a new military leadership was established, whose members included Zhou Enlai, Mao Zedong and Wang Jiaxiang – another 'Bolshevik' who gained a growing influence during the Long March.

In the weeks and months following the Zunyi Conference, Mao's strategy was repeatedly and heavily criticised. This shows that his position was far from stable. The confrontation with Zhang Guotao in the summer of 1935 brought further trouble. Zhang was not only an early CCP leader who had participated in the First Party Congress in 1921, he also commanded a larger army. If both armies had been merged, Mao would have lost influence.

Zhang Guotao was weakened by his unsuccessful march to the West. Zhu De also lost influence because of his co-operation with Zhang and late arrival in Shaanxi. Zhou Enlai and Qin Bangxian had not only been responsible for the loss of the Soviet area, they also had to take the blame for the disastrous beginning of the Long March. Even though Zhang Wentian became Party leader, he had little experience in military affairs. Chen Yun, who was in a very powerful position in 1934, left the Army during the March and went to Shanghai and, later, Moscow. Only two Politburo members survived the Long March without committing major errors or suffering serious setbacks: Liu Shaoqi and Mao Zedong. Their strength lay in the weak positions of their competitors. As Liu was not directly involved in military affairs, it was mainly Mao who profited from this situation.

FIVE

Relations between the CCP and the Communist International and the Creation of the Second United Front (1935–1938)

In Chinese and Western accounts of CCP history two main assumptions have dominated descriptions of developments after 1935:

- that Mao Zedong was the Party's unchallenged leader since the Zunyi Conference;
- that after the Long March the CCP was independent and
- that the Comintern in Moscow could hardly influence its activities.

Dick Wilson, who published one of the most detailed accounts of the Long March emphasised several 'legacies' of the March: one is the 'Supremacy of Mao' (Wilson 1971: 270), another 'Independence from Russia'. He argues:

> One of the most important consequences of the successful Long March was the guarantee which it provided that Moscow would have little sway over the Chinese Communists there after. [...] Mao was the only leader of real status who remained outside the Soviet net. (Wilson 1971: 265)

Harrison Salisbury's view of the Zunyi Conference is a more recent example:

> Nothing would be the same after Zunyi. This was the watershed – not just Mao Zedong firmly in command but a declaration of the independence of the Chinese Communist movement, independence from the overlordship of Moscow. (Salisbury 1985: 130)

A detailed analysis of the creation of the Second United Front, the Xi'an Incident and the Wang Ming's return from Moscow shows, however, that these interpretations are contradicted by developments of 1936, 1937 and 1938.

THE INTERRUPTION AND RESTORATION OF CONTACTS BETWEEN THE CCP AND THE COMINTERN

The fact that during the Long March radio communications between the CCP leadership and the Comintern in Moscow were interrupted has been known for a long time. Sixty years ago, this was already mentioned in Snow's *Red Star over China* (Snow 1937: 392). This interruption has often been interpreted as useful for Mao Zedong and negative for Qin Bangxian and Otto Braun. Braun wrote about this:

> The Central Committee's isolation was most convenient for Mao Tse-tung. It freed his hands to intensify his partisan contest for the Party leadership. (Braun 1982: 79)

At the end of the 1980s a controversy on this topic developed. In his book on Sino–Soviet relations, John Garver stressed the advantages of the interruption of radio contacts for Mao:

> Once the Long March was under way, the severance of radio contact between the CCP Politburo and the Comintern was critical to Mao's victory at the expanded Politburo conference at Zunyi in January 1935. (Garver 1988: 13)

Michael Sheng, however, argued:

> Because Mao was strongly supported by the Comintern, he was the one most worried by the loss of radio communication between the CCP headquarters and Moscow. (Sheng 1992: 151)

Concerning the reasons for the interruption and the dates of the interruption and restoration of the link, there has been confusion for several decades. It was even suggested that the CCP leadership or Mao Zedong and his supporters caused the interruption to weaken their enemies. Garver (1988a: 35) argued that 'the CCP broke off radio contact with Moscow in November 1934.'

There was, however, another reason for the interruption of radio contacts: the arrest of several communists in Shanghai and the confiscation of their radio station. As the station in the Central

Soviet in Jiangxi was not powerful enough, there had never been direct transmissions to Moscow; all messages were sent to Shanghai and then forwarded to Moscow. Braun had already argued:

> The Shanghai Central Committee Bureau's personnel were arrested by the KMT secret police and its broadcasting equipment confiscated. All communication with the Comintern Office and the ECCI was severed. The total isolation of the Central Committee from the outside world was to play an inestimable role in the further development of the Party. (Braun 1982: 79)

The exact dates of the interruption and restoration of links remained in the dark for decades.

Following Qin Bangxian's and Zhang Wentian's transfer to the Central Soviet, the two 'Bolsheviks' Li Zhusheng and Sheng Zhongliang led the Central Bureau in Shanghai. However, Li was arrested on 26 June and Sheng on 5 October 1934. The radio operators were also arrested. The last message received in the Soviet in Jiangxi was dated 16 August; there was no further contact with Shanghai and Moscow (Yao Weidou 1980: 815; Wang Jianying 1983: 222). This had nothing to do with the Long March or any decisions in Jiangxi.

After the Long March started, several attempts were made to restore the radio link. Michael Sheng described this in the following way:

> Mao took the lead to restore the channel immediately after the Zunyi Conference in January 1935, when he joined the top rank of the CCP. In early June of that year, the Party centre decided at the Ludingqiao conference to send Chen Yun and Pan Hannian to Shanghai to reestablish a radio station; both were experienced 'white-zone functionaries' with training in the Soviet Union. (Sheng 1992: 151)

Garver saw these developments differently:

> After the Zunyi conference the CCP Politburo had sent a delegation headed by Chen Yun to Moscow to report to the Comintern on developments in China and secure Moscow's support of the decisions made at Zunyi. (Garver 1988: 39)

Both descriptions are not convincing. Both emphasise a connection with the Zunyi Conference, but do not provide any sources. In Sheng's account there is also a strange gap of more than four months between 'immediately after the Zunyi Conference in January 1935' and 'early June'. We have already seen that there was no dramatic rise of Mao at Zunyi, there was no necessity to send a messenger to Moscow just to report about that conference. There are no Chinese sources indicating any initiative by Mao Zedong. David Bachman (1985: 9–10) has argued: 'Mao trusted Chen enough to assign him the delicate task of informing Wang Ming and the Comintern of the Zunyi resolutions.' But he did not provide any sources and did not explain why Mao should have trusted Chen, whom he hardly knew. In the same book, Bachman had also argued: 'Chen Yun was serving as Wang Ming's aide-de-camp [...] Chen's rise to membership in the Politburo Standing Committee was no doubt related to his position as Wang Ming's aide.' (Bachman 1985: 6).

As Chen Yun and Pan Hannian both came from the Shanghai area and had co-operated with Zhou Enlai, Wang Ming, Qin Bangxian and Zhang Wentian for many years, it is extremely unlikely that Mao sent them to Moscow. They had not entered the Jiangxi Soviet until 1933, when Qin Bangxian and Zhang Wentian also arrived (Cheng Zhongyuan 1993: 150ff.). They had relatively little contact with Mao. Sheng's claim that they were trained in the Soviet Union is not correct. Neither had left China before 1935 and had any knowledge of Russian nor do they seem to have learned any other foreign language. They were not at all suited for travelling to Moscow. It is more likely that they were only sent to Shanghai to restore the local Party organisation and prepare the resumption of radio contacts. If the dispatch of messengers to Moscow had already been planned during the Long March, it is more likely that people with a good knowledge of Russian, or at least English, would have been chosen.

Pan Hannian left the Red Army in Guizhou. On 5 March the Party leadership had received a message from Ren Bishi with information on the destruction of the CCP organisation in Shanghai. Pan was ordered by Zhang Wentian to re-establish the organisation in Shanghai and to restore radio contacts with the Comintern. Pan travelled via Guiyang, Liuzhou and Hong Kong to Shanghai (Cheng Zhongyuan 1993: 216). Chen Yun participated in the crossing of the Luding Bridge in June and then left the Army. At that time, there was no news from Shanghai. Therefore the Party leadership also sent Chen. Chen travelled through Sichuan to Shanghai (Lü Cheng 1991: 106). Because of the numerous arrests of CCP members, Pan and Chen were not able to create a stable Party organisation or run a radio station. As they could not work in Shanghai and did not feel safe, they decided to go to Moscow, where the Seventh Comintern Congress was held; there are no sources indicating that this step was planned before their arrival in Shanghai. Chen and Pan left Shanghai in August together with some other Chinese Communists (Cheng Zhongyuan 1993: 216ff.).

THE COMINTERN'S NEW POLICY AND ITS TRANSMISSION TO CHINA

After the loss of radio contact with the CCP in the autumn of 1934, the Comintern in Moscow made several attempts to restore communications. With the propagation of its new united front policy and the opening of its Seventh Congress, it was even more important to inform the Chinese communists about Moscow's strategy. The Comintern sent several messengers to China, but because of difficult transport conditions and attacks by warlord armies and bandits it was very difficult to reach the CCP; in addition, the Long March had not finished at that time and nobody knew where the Red Army was going. In April 1935 Yan Hongyan, who had been sent from Shanghai to Moscow in July 1934, was sent by the Comintern to China. Yan travelled through Xinjiang and Xi'an to Wayaobao, where he arrived in December 1935 (Pang Xianzhi 1993: 1/502). Liu Changsheng left Moscow at about the same time, but did not reach Wayaobao until May 1936. There are also reports about a group of seven men, who were trying to carry a radio station to China, but were attacked by bandits. (Braun 1973: 210)

After Yan Hongyan's and Liu Changsheng's departure, the Comintern, which was preparing its Seventh Congress, decided on further changes in its strategy. It now advocated a united front policy for several countries, including China. To propagate this policy, the 'Resolution of 1 August' was formulated in Moscow and then published – with some delay. Even though the resolution was drafted by the Comintern, Moscow tried to create the impression that it was passed by the CCP leadership in China, and then transmitted to Europe (Xiang Qing 1994: 396–397). For decades, this interpretation was repeated in Chinese and Western publications and it was argued that the CCP leadership in China took the initiative for a United Front with the KMT. As the Red Army was still on the Long March and passed through the place Maoergai in August, the resolution was associated with a conference there. Ironically, in the autumn of 1935, this resolution became known to the whole world (including the KMT capital Nanjing), before the CCP leadership in Northwest China heard about it (Kataoka 1974: 20–22; Fang Xiao 1991: 523–525).

To inform the CCP about the Seventh Congress and the August Resolution, the Comintern sent Lin Yuying (a relative of Lin Biao) – also known as Lin Zhongdan and Zhang Hao – to China. Lin left Moscow in August 1935 and reached the CCP leadership in Wayaobao in November 1935 – before Yan Hongyan and Liu Changsheng arrived. Lin first met Zhang Wentian, Deng Fa and Li Weihan and, shortly afterwards, Mao Zedong. At the Wayaobao Conference (17–25 December) Lin's report on the Comintern congress was discussed in detail. But, for security reasons, Lin did not bring any documents. Thus he could only provide a general summary of the August Resolution (Braun 1973: 210–211; Yang Yunruo 1988: 375; Xiang Qing 1994: 396–397).

These activities prove that the Comintern made numerous attempts to push through its united front strategy accepted by the Seventh Congress and was very active in propagating the 'Resolution of 1 August', sending messengers to China and restore radio contacts. As a result of Lin Yuying's arrival, the CCP leadership had a basic idea about the new Comintern strategy and, in the following spring, radio contacts were also restored.

PREPARATIONS FOR THE SECOND UNITED FRONT

Following the arrival of the Red Army in Shaanxi in Autumn 1935, the CCP, the KMT and the Comintern in Moscow made numerous attempts to establish new contacts to counter the Japanese threat; these activities led to the 'Second United Front'. Even though conditions and aims were different, it was modelled after the First United Front of the years 1924–1927. The early preparations for the Second United Front, particularly the months before the Xi'an Incident of December 1936, have never been described in detail. Difficult problems have to be solved. Communist leaders in China (CCP) and Moscow (Comintern) and Kuomintang leaders in

Figure 6: The leadership of the Communist International in 1935. *Front row, from left to right:* G. Dimitrov, P. Togliatti, W. Florin, Wang Ming; *back row:* O. W. Kuusinen, K. Gottwald, W. Pieck and D. S. Manuilski.

Nanjing (Chiang Kai-shek, etc.) and Xi'an (Zhang Xueliang, Yang Hucheng) held very different views. Even within the CCP leadership in Yan'an and the Kuomintang leadership in Nanjing there was no unity. As the early negotiations were oral and secret, there are very few reliable documents. Another problem is that after the break-up of the united front, neither side was interested in discussing or documenting its origins. Only with the new attempts of CCP–KMT co-operation starting around 1980, was the history of earlier united action studied again.

What is interesting for the topic discussed in this book is the question of whether the establishment of the Second United Front was a result of CCP policy and independence or a consequence of Comintern or Soviet strategy and dominance.

In the autumn and winter of 1935–36 all sides were interested in some kind of co-operation. The CCP leadership in Wayaobao was mainly interested in a ceasefire and co-operation with the generals Zhang Xueliang and Yang Hucheng in Xi'an. Some members of the Kuomintang leadership in Nanjing were interested in co-operation with the CCP and improved relations with the Soviet Union. The Soviet leadership advocated co-operation of the Kuomintang and CCP in China, and wanted to improve Soviet relations with the KMT in Nanjing.

There were at least four attempts by the KMT to contact the CCP. In November 1935, Song Ziwen, a leading member of the KMT and brother of Song Qingling, contacted the communist Zhou Xiao-zhou with the help of the deputy minister of railways, Zeng Yangfu. Because of considerable delay caused by several trips by Zhou between Peking and Nanjing, this did not lead to significant results (Quanguo Zhonggong dangshi yanjiuhui 1987: 79–82).

Several weeks later, Song Ziwen and Song Qingling asked their friend Dong Jianwu, who was an underground CCP activist known as Pastor Wang, to deliver a message to the CCP leadership in the Northwest. Dong reached Wayaobao at the end of February and soon brought a reply to the KMT in Nanjing (Quanguo Zhonggong dangshi yanjiuhui 1987: 82–83).

At the same time, a friend of the deputy railway minister Zeng Yangfu contacted another communist called Zhang Zihua, who also took a message to Wayaobao (Quanguo Zhonggong dangshi yanjiu-hui 1987: 83–87).

These and other activities show that the KMT made several serious attempts to establish contact with the CCP leadership. However, no communist attempts to contact Nanjing are known.

In addition to these attempts in China, the KMT also tried to contact communists in Moscow. In December 1935, Chen Lifu took a boat from China to Europe, to start negotiations in Moscow. For decades, the details of this mission remained unknown. Quoting a Chinese source, the American historian Garver argued:

> According to Xiang Qing, Chen [Lifu] still had full pleni-potentiary powers to negotiate an agreement when he arrived in Moscow. Although Chen remained in the Soviet capital for

several weeks, Stalin was unwilling either to meet with him or to express his opinions on Sino–Soviet relations to other Chinese diplomats. (Garver 1988a: 45)

This strange description is, however, the result of a translation error. The Chinese text was a translation from a well-known American book by O. E. Clubb, which said:

> He arrived in Berlin and then, instead of proceeding to Moscow to present his full powers and the Chinese proposals, waited for word from Stalin agreeing to the negotiations. The cagey Stalin sent no word, and Ch'en returned home in April. (Clubb 1971: 278)

In fact, Chen was told to return to China and never arrived in Moscow. Chen Lifu himself wrote that he secretly travelled to Berlin (via Marseille), but was recalled by Chiang Kai-shek before proceeding to Moscow. This was mainly caused by Chinese and Soviet fears, that the Japanese might find out about Sino–Soviet contacts and use these as a pretext for military actions (Chen Lifu 1987: 94). In addition, in early 1936, the KMT had already contacted the CCP in Moscow. The KMT military attaché Deng Wenyi, a former student of Sun Yat-sen University, who knew Chiang Kai-shek and Wang Ming, started talks soon after his arrival in Moscow. On 13 January 1936 he met Pan Hannian (see above) and, shortly afterwards, Wang Ming. There were no direct results, but Wang suggested that Deng should travel to Shaanxi to negotiate with the CCP. When Pan Hannian prepared his return to China in April, he again met Deng Wenyi, who told him to proceed to Nanjing and contact Chen Guofu, the brother of Chen Lifu (Quanguo Zhonggong dangshi yanjiuhui 1987: 78–79).

The above-mentioned examples show that in the autumn of 1935, the KMT leadership in Nanjing took the initiative to negotiate with the CCP. At that time, the CCP leadership wanted to co-operate with the generals Zhang Xueliang and Yang Hucheng in Xi'an to fight Chiang Kai-shek.

THE XI'AN INCIDENT

The arrest of KMT leader Chiang Kai-shek by his generals Zhang Xueliang and Yang Hucheng on 12 December 1936, which became famous as the Xi'an Incident, is well-known and need not be described in detail (see Harrison 1972: 268–270; Ch'en 1986: 226–229). The fact that Mao opposed the release of Chiang, but submitted to Comintern demands for Chiang's release, has also been known for decades. This outcome shows, that in 1936, Mao's position within the CCP leadership was not as strong as has been thought. The first reaction of the CCP leadership to the capture of Chiang, the reaction to the Comintern demands and the following actions of CCP leaders, show clearly that the CCP was not independent and accepted Comintern orders, even when it completely disagreed.

In his *Comintern Agent in China*, Otto Braun emphasised that Mao 'could not have his way':

> Literally overnight there occurred a sudden turn-about which [...] was impelled by a radio message from [...] Moscow. It was even rumoured that Stalin had personally intervened and sent Mao Tse-tung an ultimatum. [...] The Politburo hastily convened. [...] It was decided to drop the demand that Chiang Kaishek be tried before a people's court. [...] What cannot be doubted is that Mao Tse-tung endeavoured to force his sectarian, adventurist policy on the ECCI and continued to defend it after the radio message had been received. [...] Mao did not reverse his position until he realised that he could not have his way. (Braun 1982: 187)

Edgar Snow described Mao's reaction to the Comintern instructions in more drastic words:

> Mao Tse-tung flew into a rage when the order came from Moscow to release Chiang. Mao swore and stamped his feet. Until then they had planned to give Chiang a public trial and to organise a Northwest anti-Japanese defense government. (Snow 1957: 2)

For a long time the 'peaceful solution' of the conflict was described as a harmonious decision by the CCP leadership, but recent publications discuss the contradictions within the Politburo and the differences with Moscow (Yang Yunruo 1988: 386–395; Cheng Zhongyuan 1993: 344–350; Pang Xianzhi 1993: 1/ 620–630).

WANG MING'S ARRIVAL IN YAN'AN AND THE DECEMBER CONFERENCE

In the autumn of 1937, Wang Ming's return to China led to a drastic change in the balance of power. After his departure from Shanghai in the autumn of 1931, Wang had spent six years in Moscow and worked for the Communist International. In contrast to most other members of the CCP leadership he had neither visited the Chinese Soviet districts nor participated in the Long March. Therefore many leading communists did not know him personally until 1937. After the Comintern had for several years sent only radio messages and little-known messengers, Wang Ming was a member of the Presidium of the Executive Committee of the Comintern (ECCI) and simultaneously a CCP Politburo member. This was also Wang's first direct confrontation with Mao Zedong, who had not met him before (Kampen 1989c: 82–97).

For Wang Ming's return to China, different dates have been suggested, which have led to considerable confusion. Warren Kuo

Figure 7: The participants of the 'December Conference' in 1937. *Front row, from left to right:* Xiang Ying, He Kequan, Wang Ming, Chen Yun, Liu Shaoqi; *back row:* Kang Sheng, Peng Dehuai, Zhang Wentian, Zhang Guotao, Lin Boqu, Qin Bangxian, Zhou Enlai and Mao Zedong.

(1970: 326), Otto Braun (1982: 218), Gregor Benton (1975: 77) and Lyman Van Slyke (1986: 616) gave October 1937 as the month of Wang's arrival. Several authors (e.g. Braun 1982: 219) highlighted the 'surprising' differences between Wang's position and Mao's speech *The Situation and Tasks in the Anti-Japanese War after the Fall of Shanghai and Taiyuan* (Mao 1937: 2/61–74) of 12 November. Van Slyke commented on the conference of 12 November: 'First meeting attended by Wang Ming, just returned from Moscow' (Van Slyke 1986: 611). If this had been the case, Mao would have openly and publicly contradicted the policies of Wang Ming and the Comintern.

Zhang Guotao, however, gave the 'last ten days of December' as the date of Wang's arrival (Chang 1972: 565), Guillermaz (1972: 366) early 1938. But these dates would contradict Wang's participation in an important Politburo conference which lasted from 9 to 14 December (see below).

Wang Ming, in fact, left Moscow on 14 November 1937 and reached Yan'an – after stops in Dihua (Urumqi) and Lanzhou – on 29 November, two weeks after Mao's above-mentioned speech and before the Politburo conference (Wang 1979: 48; Cao Zhongbin 1991: 444).

On his way from Moscow to Yan'an, Wang Ming was accompanied by Meng Qingshu, Kang Sheng, Wu Kejian and Zeng Shan. In addition, Chen Yun joined the group in Xinjiang. The importance of the visitors was demonstrated by the fact, that they were the first representatives of the Comintern to arrive in Yan'an by plane, which was a rare event in that poor, isolated area.

With the arrival of Wang Ming, Kang Sheng and Chen Yun, three powerful Politburo members, who had been abroad for several years, again participated in the Party leadership and changed the balance of power.

On 9 December, about two weeks after their arrival, an important Politburo meeting was opened, which became known as the 'December Conference'. This was the most complete meeting of CCP leaders since the Fourth Plenum in 1931. They represented the most important groups within the Party. In November, Xiang Ying, who had been an opponent of Mao in the early 1930s, but did not participate in the Long March, also arrived in Yan'an.

Of the thirteen participants of the December Conference, Mao Zedong, Zhang Wentian, Zhou Enlai, Chen Yun, Qin Bangxian, Lin Boqu, Peng Dehuai, He Kequan and Liu Shaoqi had taken part in the Long March; Zhang Guotao had participated in the March of the Fourth Army; Xiang Ying had stayed in South China between 1934 and 1937; Wang Ming and Kang Sheng had spent several years in Moscow (Wang Xiuxin 1992: 200).

Following the opening speech by Zhang Wentian, Wang Ming transmitted the most recent Comintern instructions and presented a long report on ways to achieve the victory in the Anti-Japanese War. He encouraged closer co-operation with Chiang Kai-shek and criticised the decisions of the Luochuan Conference (August 1937) and Mao's speech of 12 November. Different sources indicate that the majority of Politburo members supported Wang's line. On 11 November, three days before his departure from Moscow, Wang had been received by Stalin and Dimitrov and Wang saw himself as their representative (Cao Zhongbin 1991: 444).

Zhang Guotao described his behaviour in the following way:

> Wang Ming was like an 'imperial envoy' from Moscow holding high the emperor's double-edged sword, his manner of speech resembling that of an imperial envoy transmitting an imperial decree. (Chang 1972: 572)

But opposition by Mao Zedong and Zhang Wentian is said to have prevented the acceptance of Wang's report as an official Politburo resolution (Yang Yunruo 1988: 437–442; Cheng Zhongyuan 1993: 399–402).

Within the Party leadership, Mao's position was considerably weakened as the three newcomers were not only Politburo members, but also entered the Secretariat – none of them supported Mao's policies. During the conference, a preparatory committee for the CCP's Seventh Party congress was established. It included 25 members, five of whom formed a Secretariat: Mao Zedong, Wang Ming, Kang Sheng, Chen Yun and Zhang Wentian. Mao became chairman and Wang Ming secretary. In this committee Mao's position was also weak. Only Zhang Wentian supported him and the newcomers had a majority (Wang Jianying 1983: 296; Pang Xianzhi 1993: 2/40–41).

The Politburo assigned responsibility for united front work to Wang Ming, who was thus responsible for negotiations with the KMT. Another important decision of the December Conference was the establishment of a Central China Bureau in Wuhan, where the

KMT government resided after the Japanese occupation of Nanjing. Shortly after the conference, Wang Ming travelled to Wuhan and met Chiang Kai-shek (Cao Zhongbin 1991: 296–302).

In the 1970s, Otto Braun had already indicated that the Wuhan office had not just been a subordinate regional bureau:

> We called this office the 'second Politburo'. [...] While the Central Office [in Wuhan] implemented the united front line approved in December 1937 and affirmed by the ECCI, Mao Tse-tung pursued his own ends in Yenan. [...] Po Ku [Qin Bangxian] and Chou En-lai [Zhou Enlai] seemed to hedge between Mao and Wang, whereas Hsiang Ying [Xiang Ying] steadfastly stood by the latter's policies in the Central Committee. [...] Mao devoted most of the first half of 1938 to the theoretical distillation and generalisation of his views on the strategy of revolutionary war. (Braun 1982: 223–225)

The weakening of Mao's position following the return of Wang Ming was confirmed by many different sources. Li Weihan, who had already known Mao before the founding of the CCP, stated in his memoirs: 'For about half a year Mao was in a minority and sometimes completely isolated.' (Li Weihan 1986: 443). A footnote to Mao's above-mentioned speech of 12 November in his *Selected Works* says that his views 'met with immediate opposition from the Right opportunists in the Party, and not until the Sixth Plenary Session of the Sixth Central Committee in October 1938 was the Right deviation basically overcome.' (Mao 1968: 2/61). Mao himself said in a recently published speech at the Seventh Party congress of 1945: 'Since the Zunyi Conference the guiding line of the Central Committee has been correct, but there have also been setbacks. The December Conference at the beginning of the Anti-Japanese War was such a setback.' (Mao Zedong 1945: 32).

As the 'peaceful solution' of the Xi'an Incident, the arrival of Wang Ming in Yan'an also demonstrates that Mao Zedong had no majority in the Politburo, and that the Comintern continued to intervene successfully in CCP politics.

THE MARCH CONFERENCE AND REN BISHI'S TRIP TO MOSCOW

As the December Conference had not produced a political resolution supporting their line, Wang Ming and Zhou Enlai soon

Figure 8: The CCP leadership in early 1938. *From left to right*: Zhang Wentian, Kang Sheng, Zhou Enlai, He Kequan, Wang Ming Mao Zedong, Ren Bishi and Zhang Guotao.

suggested the opening of another Politburo conference. In a telegram to the Politburo of 24 February 1938 they demanded that,

a Politburo meeting should be held,

it should last for two days,

Wang and Zhou should represent the Wuhan office and return to Wuhan immediately afterwards,

more leading cadres should be sent to Wuhan. (Jue Shi 1988: 17)

Mao is said to have been very upset about these instructions from Wuhan (Jue Shi 1988: 17). Still, the conference took place as planned. It started on 27 February and ended on 1 March 1938 and became known as the March Conference. The following Politburo members took part: Mao Zedong, Wang Ming, Zhang Wentian, Zhou Enlai, Kang Sheng, He Kequan, Ren Bishi, Zhang Guotao (Wang Jin 1992: 205). On 27 Wang Ming delivered the main report. On the following day there were speeches by Mao Zedong,

Zhou Enlai, Zhang Guotao and Zhang Wentian. On 1 March, Wang Ming presented a long summary of the conference. (After his return to Wuhan, Wang Ming published an unauthorised summary of the Politburo meeting.) During the conference, Mao demanded that Wang should stay in Yan'an and not return to Wuhan, but did not succeed with this plan. Wang received the support of Zhou Enlai, Kang Sheng, He Kequan and Zhang Guotao (Cao Zhongbin 1991: 303–307). In this controversy, Mao was supported by Ren Bishi and Zhang Wentian, who had opposed him in the early 1930s (Wang Xiuxin 1992: 200–211; Pang Xianzhi 1993: 2/51).

THE COMINTERN AND THE SIXTH PLENUM

Because of its inability to agree on a policy, the Politburo decided to send Ren Bishi to Moscow to inform the Comintern about the situation in China and seek its advice (Yang Yunruo 1988: 448). In March 1938, Ren Bishi travelled to Moscow. After Wang Ming's departure from Moscow, Wang Jiaxiang had represented the CCP at the Comintern. As he wanted to return to China, Ren Bishi succeeded him. At a Comintern meeting on 14 April, Ren Bishi reported on the situation in China. On 11 June the ECCI Presidium passed two resolutions on China, one remained secret, the other was published (Yang Yunruo 1988: 446–458; Zhang Xuexin 1994: 422–434). Shortly afterwards, the general secretary of the Comintern, Dimitrov, met Ren and Wang Jiaxiang, who was planning to return to China. According to Wang, Dimitrov told them that Mao Zedong should be acknowledged as the leader of the Chinese Revolution and that Wang Ming should not compete for the leadership (Wang Jiaxiang xuanji bianjizu 1989: 138–142; Xu Zehao 1991: 110–112).

Wang Jiaxiang left Moscow in July 1938 and must have arrived in Yan'an by early August. On 3 August he was appointed head of the political department of the Eighth Route Army. At the same time, the convening of an enlarged Politburo meeting was announced for the following month (Pang Xianzhi 1993: 2/84–85). At a Politburo meeting on 14 September, Wang Jiaxiang transmitted a Comintern directive and Dimitrov's message (Wang Jiaxiang xuanji bianjizu 1989: 138–142). When Wang Ming was told about the upcoming meeting, he first refused to travel from Wuhan to Yan'an, and demanded that the Party leadership should meet in the KMT capital

Wuhan. After Yan'an refused, Wang Ming and Zhou Enlai finally went to Yan'an. On 26 September the Politburo decided, that Mao Zedong should present the main report at the upcoming Sixth Plenum (Cao Zhongbin 1991: 318–320; Pang Xianzhi 1993: 2/90–91).

Li Weihan remarked:

> When Comrade Wang Jiaxiang came back from the Comintern he transmitted Dimitroff's instructions. The most important, most decisive sentence was: 'Dimitroff said, that Comrade Mao Zedong is the leader of the Chinese people.' [...] I heard that the Politburo originally asked Wang Ming to give the report. But then his draft was not accepted, and instead Chairman Mao was asked to do it. (Li Weihan 1987: 641–642)

The alleged directive of Dimitrov, which is not yet confirmed by reliable documents, on the one hand indicates that Wang Ming still had a strong position and, on the other, that he was no longer supported by Dimitrov. It is not known, what Dimitrov really said and whether he was representing the Comintern or Stalin (Kampen 1989b: 714–715).

Table 15: Participants of the Sixth Plenum (1938)

Politburo: members and alternate members	Mao Zedong, Zhu De, Zhou Enlai, **Wang Ming, Zhang Wentian,** Xiang Ying, **Qin Bangxian,** Kang Sheng, **Wang Jiaxiang,** Peng Dehuai, Liu Shaoqi, Chen Yun
Other Central Committee members and alternate members	Guan Xiangying, Zhang Hao, **Yang Shangkun,** Li Fuchun, Li Weihan
Other participants	about 35, including: He Long, Deng Xiaoping, Luo Ronghuan, Peng Zhen, Pan Hannian, Xu Teli, Zeng Shan, Wu Yuzhang

Note: '28 Bolsheviks' = **bold**
(Source: Wang Xiuxin 1993: 231)

The Sixth Plenum of the Sixth Central Committee was in many ways unusual (see Kampen 1989c: 88–91). It was the first Plenum for five years, since the Long March and the Zunyi Conference, and since the return of Wang Ming, Kang Sheng, Chen Yun and Wang

Figure 9: Politburo members participating in the Sixth Plenum. *Front row, from left to right:* Kang Sheng, Mao Zedong, Wang Jiaxiang, Zhu De, Xiang Ying, Wang Ming; *back row:* Chen Yun, Qin Bangxian, Peng Dehuai, Liu Shaoqi, Zhou Enlai and Zhang Wentian.

Jiaxiang from Moscow. Here, a legal reorganisation of the leadership – and a promotion of Mao Zedong – according to Party statutes could have taken place. But this did not happen (Wang Xiuxin 1993: 228ff.).

Mao Zedong's position was strengthened by the Sixth Plenum, but this was mainly due to factors beyond his control:

Wang Jiaxiang's proclamation of Comintern support for Mao.

The loss of Wuhan and, thus, the failure of the united front strategy of Wang Ming, Qin Bangxian and Zhou Enlai. This not only weakened Wang, Qin and Zhou, but also their allies Xiang Ying and He Kequan.

However, the strengthening of Mao's position and the weakening of that of his opponents was still not strong enough to cause a reorganisation of the leadership. In the Politburo, Mao was still in a minority. For the following four years, this situation continued. Mao was not promoted, his opponents were not demoted or dismissed, (Pang Xianzhi 1993: 2/91–95) and there was no open criticism of Wang Ming, Qin Bangxian or Zhou Enlai.

SUMMARY

The analysis of CCP–Comintern relations in the three years after the Long March (autumn 1935 to autumn 1938) shows that the Comintern still exercised a strong influence on the CCP leadership. The CCP practised the Comintern's United Front strategy, laid down at the Seventh World Congress in 1935. The CCP leadership accepted Moscow's view on the Xi'an Incident and, reluctantly, agreed to the release of Chiang Kai-shek. After Wang Ming's return to China in the autumn of 1937, the CCP also supported Wang's interpretation of the Comintern's strategy. Finally, the Comintern's withdrawal of support for Wang Ming was the decisive factor in the promotion of Mao Zedong. These developments show that during these years the CCP was not yet independent and that Mao was often in a minority position and far from an 'unchallenged' leader.

When the Red Army reached Northern Shaanxi in the autumn of 1935, Mao's strength lay in the weakness of several Politburo members (Qin Bangxian, Zhou Enlai) and the physical absence of others (Chen Yun, Zhang Guotao, Wang Ming, Kang Sheng). Zhang

Figure 10: Zhou Enlai in the late 1930s.

Guotao had weakened his position by his disastrous march to the West and the loss of most of his army; he left Yan'an and the CCP in 1938. Wang Ming's return in 1937 was a more serious threat to Mao. Wang Ming, Kang Sheng and Chen Yun were not only three powerful rivals; after their return they were also supported by Qin Bangxian, He Kequan and Zhou Enlai, who had reluctantly co-operated with Mao in the preceding years. In early 1938 Mao was quite isolated and there were no indications of a comeback. He did, however, profit from a change in the Comintern's attitude and from the strength of Japanese troops. The loss of Wuhan in the autumn of 1938 ruined the united front strategy pursued by Wang Ming and his supporters. As in 1934, when the Jiangxi Soviet was lost, Zhou Enlai and Qin Bangxian had to accept responsibility for a major defeat. The Politburo members who stayed in Yan'an during the Wuhan crisis (Wang Jiaxiang, Kang Sheng and Chen Yun) profited from the weakness of their colleagues and began to support Mao. The Sixth Plenum in the autumn of 1938, however, also showed that Mao's position was not as strong as has been claimed for many decades. He did not become Party chairman or general secretary. If he had suffered defeats as Wang Ming or Zhou Enlai did in Wuhan or if Wang and Zhou had achieved major successes in the following years, Mao might never have become chairman of the CCP.

SIX

The Yan'an Rectification Movement and the Evolution of a New CCP Leadership (1940–1945)

In the preceding chapters it has been shown that Mao Zedong did not become head of the CCP in 1935 or in the following three years. From 1938 the Party had a collective leadership without a general secretary or chairman. The power struggle was still going on. In this chapter the analysis will focus on the 1940s, when Mao finally became Party chairman.

It has also been shown that after 1935 the Comintern still exerted great influence on the CCP leadership. In the following paragraphs it will be discussed, whether this was also true for the early 1940s.

THE CCP LEADERSHIP IN THE EARLY YEARS OF THE WAR AGAINST THE JAPANESE

In the first two years after the Sixth Plenum of autumn 1938, there were no significant changes in the composition of the Party leadership. After the Sixth Plenum, Mao was in a stronger position than in the preceding months, but was not promoted. Within the Politburo and among the heads of the CC departments, Mao did not have a majority. Until the early 1940s, he had not published very much. In contrast to Wang Ming and Zhou Enlai, he had no contact with highranking KMT politicians or Comintern leaders.

Wang Ming was weakened, but was neither dismissed from the Party leadership, nor publicly criticised. He was a member of the Central Committee, Politburo and Secretariat and headed the CC United Front Department. In Wuhan and in Chongqing he was a member of the National Political Consultative Assembly and belonged to the Secretariat of the Executive Committee of the Communist International. Between 1938 and 1940 he published dozens of articles in several CCP journals. In 1938 he had already published his *Selected Works* in Wuhan and, in 1940, his pamphlet on the Bolshevisation of the CCP of 1931 was reprinted in Yan'an (Cao Zhongbin 1991: 448ff.).

Qin Bangxian, one of Wang's closest allies, also stayed in the CC and Politburo. In 1939 and 1940 he worked in the CCP's Chongqing office and headed the Xinhua News Agency. In the spring of 1941 he moved to Yan'an, and became head of the newly established official CCP organ *Jiefang Ribao (Liberation Daily)*. Zhang Wentian and He Kequan, the 'Bolshevik', who severely criticised Mao at the Zunyi Conference, headed the CC Propaganda Department; in the autumn of 1941, He Kequan was also made secretary of the committee for youth work. Kang Sheng and Chen Yun had closely co-operated with Wang Ming in Shanghai, later went to Moscow and returned with Wang Ming in November 1937; they now headed the CC departments for Social Affairs (State security) and Organisation (Kampen 1993: 302–309). Zhou Enlai headed the CCP's Southern Bureau (Nanfangju) in the provisional KMT capital Chongqing (Wang Jianying 1983: 330ff.). Until 1941, there was no dismissal or demotion of the 'Bolsheviks' and their allies.

MAO ZEDONG AND THE CONTROVERSY OVER CCP HISTORY

In early 1941, there were important changes within the CCP leadership. The South-Anhui Incident, in which KMT troops attacked the communist New Fourth Army, was a heavy blow for the CCP and damaged Wang Ming's position in two ways: on the one hand, his strategy of close co-operation with the KMT again failed, on the other hand, he lost an important ally in the Politburo when Xiang Ying was killed in March.

On 19 May 1941 Mao gave a speech, which became known as *Reform our study*, and included criticism of the Party's 'style in work', which was often repeated in the Rectification Movement.

In Chinese and in Western accounts of CCP history, the Yan'an Rectification Movement plays an important role. Most scholars regard February 1942 when Mao Zedong gave his famous speech *Rectify the Party's style in work*, as the beginning of the movement (Compton 1952: xxxiv; Kuo 1971: 557; Uhalley 1988: 58).

For the power struggle within the leadership, the enlarged Politburo meeting of the autumn of 1941 was more important; this was the real beginning of rectification, but this meeting was kept secret for decades. Raymond F. Wylie commented:

> Unfortunately, as James Harrison has pointed out [1972: 336] 'virtually nothing' is known of this meeting of the enlarged Polit-buro. We do know, however, that the session was of unusual import-ance. (Wylie 1980: 166)

In 1986 Lyman Van Slyke wrote in his contribution to the *Cambridge History of China*:

> Unfortunately, none of the documents of this very significant meeting are presently available and little is known about it. (Van Slyke 1986: 687)

Since the middle of the 1980s, several articles and documents have been published in China, which provide some information about this conference (see Kampen 1989b: 716ff.).

The conference began on 10 September and was later called 'September Conference'; but it ended only on 22 October. The Politburo members Mao Zedong, Ren Bishi, Wang Ming, Zhang Wentian, Chen Yun, Wang Jiaxiang, He Kequan, Qin Bangxian, Deng Fa, Zhu De and Kang Sheng participated and Yang Shangkun, Li Fuchun, Lin Boqu, Gao Gang, Ye Jianying, Li Weihan and Hu Qiaomu were also present. Among the Politburo members only Zhou Enlai, Liu Shaoqi and Peng Dehuai, who were not in Yan'an, were missing (Wang Yifan 1988: 27).

On 10 September 1941, Mao Zedong gave a speech on CCP history in the 1930s. The outline of this speech was published 44 years later in an internal journal as *Fighting Subjectivism and Faction-alism;* in 1993 it was included in a new edition of Mao's works, commemorating his hundredth birthday (Mao Zedong 1941). This is the earliest available document of Mao, which discusses internal power struggles of the 1930s in detail. This speech was the beginning of a long controversy concerning CCP history, which ended only in 1953 with the publication of the *Resolution on some questions in the history of Our Party.*

In his speech Mao criticised the line of the Party between 1932 and 1935. He criticised several incorrect decisions and actions of this period; these included the campaign against the 'Luo Ming line' (see Chapter 3), in which, in 1933, his brother Mao Zetan, Deng Xiaoping and others were attacked. One remarkable aspect of Mao's speech is that, in contrast to the later official accounts, he argued that the beginning of the negative phase was in 1932. This year was not important as far as Wang Ming was concerned, as Wang spent these years in the Soviet Union and never entered the Jiangxi Soviet. In this text of 1941 Mao does not discuss the Fourth Plenum of 1931, or the rise of Wang Ming and Qin Bangxian. These events were only emphasized in the later stages of the movement. However, in 1932, Zhou Enlai entered the Soviet and took over the leadership. In the same year, Mao was dismissed from the military command (Ningdu Conference). Zhou Enlai was also a leading activist in the campaign against the 'Luo Ming line'.

In his speech, Mao also argued that the incorrect line had not been completely corrected at the Zunyi Conference of 1935 and the Sixth Plenum of 1938 and that subjectivism and dogmatism still dominated in Yan'an. To overcome these problems Mao suggested a number of measures, including the study of CC Documents passed since the last (Sixth) Party congress in 1928. Therefore a Central Study Group should be established, which would be led by Mao Zedong and Wang Jiaxiang (Mao Zedong 1941: 1–6).

Already on 8 September, the CC Secretariat had decided to establish a Politburo study group – under the leadership of Mao Zedong and Wang Jiaxiang – to analyse CCP documents of the 1930s. On 26 September, the CC passed the 'Resolution on high-level study groups' and established the Central Study Group with Mao Zedong as chairman and Wang Jiaxiang as vice-chairman. On 13 October the Secretariat established a five-member committee (Mao Zedong, Wang Jiaxiang, Ren Bishi, Kang Sheng and Peng Zhen) to investigate Party history. Mao Zedong became chairman and Wang Jiaxiang was asked to draft a document on Party history. This document can be regarded as the first of numerous drafts of the *Resolution on some questions in the history of Our Party*, passed in 1945 and published in 1953 (Feng Hui 1986: 11; Pang Xianzhi 1993: 2/326–328).

The document collection since the Sixth Congress

In connection with the controversy on CCP history, Mao Zedong and Wang Jiaxiang supervised the compilation of more than 500 Party documents of the years 1928–1941. This collection, the first comprehensive edition of CCP Documents in Party history, was printed in December 1941 and titled *Since the Sixth Party Congress – Secret Party Documents (Liu Da yilai – Dangnei mimi wenjian)*. Until the 1980s, it was the basis for most collections of CCP documents printed in the People's Republic of China. Even though this compilation was reprinted in 1952 and 1980, for many decades there has been great confusion about the contents of the original version of 1941. Mao Zedong's former private secretary, Hu Qiaomu (1912–1992), described the origins of the compilation in his posthumously published memoirs. According to Hu, 519 documents of the period June 1928 to November 1941 were included. Only 500 numbered and classified copies were printed and distributed to Party and Army institutions, but not to individuals. When Yan'an was attacked by the enemy in 1947 and the CCP leadership left, most copies were destroyed. The few surviving copies are still kept secret. Most references to and quotes from the collection are referring to the reprints of 1952 and 1980, which were not identical with the original version. The main difference is the treatment of Mao Zedong's texts. In the original version of 1941 only very few texts by Mao were included. In the 1952 and 1980 reprints there is a note saying that the texts by Mao, which were included in his *Selected Works*, were not reprinted and that only their titles would be given in the table of contents of the reprints. The large number of Mao texts in the table of contents now created the impression that they had all been included in the 1941 collection. But this was not the case. The tables of contents just included many of the titles of texts in Mao's *Selected Works* which had not been included in the 1941 edition (Hu Qiaomu 1994: 175–182).

Because many Chinese and most foreign scholars did not have access to the original version of 1941 and the reprint of 1952, they often – on the basis of the 1980 edition – assumed that texts by Mao already dominated the 1941 edition and incorrectly concluded that these texts played an important role in rectification.

The large collection of 1941 was also the basis of later selections of CCP documents, such as *Documents of the Rectification movement (Zhengfeng wenxian)*, *Two Lines (Liangtiao luxian)*, *Selected Works of Mao Zedong (Mao Zedong xuanji)*, and most of the collections of CCP documents published in the 1950s, 1960s and 1970s.

THE RECTIFICATION MOVEMENT AND MAO ZEDONG'S
RISE TO THE LEADERSHIP

The above-mentioned preparations and the compilation of Party documents in the autumn of 1941 was followed, in February 1942, by the main phase of the rectification movement. This has been repeatedly described since Compton published the translations of important documents of the movement in 1952, and will not be repeated here. (See Selden 1971; Harrison 1972; Teiwes 1976; Seybolt 1986.)

However, even though the Yan'an rectification movement played an important role in Western studies of CCP history, only the economic and military background, the controversies in literature and art, as well as education, indoctrination, purges and 'terror' were analysed. As most scholars assumed that Mao Zedong had already taken over the Party leadership in the 1930s, this aspect of the rectification movement was not studied in detail. Selden just wrote: 'Mao increased his prestige as a party and national leader' (Selden 1971: 198); Teiwes mentioned the consolidation of Mao's position (Teiwes 1976: 15). More recently, however, Patricia Stranahan has described the fight for control of the *Liberation Daily* as the 'Last Battle' between 'Mao and the Internationalists' (Stranahan 1990: 521) and concluded that 'Mao's rise and the Internationalists fall' was clearly evident 'by 1943' (ibid.: 536).

From 16 to 20 March 1943, Mao Zedong, Liu Shaoqi, Ren Bishi, Zhu De, Kang Sheng, He Kequan, Qin Bangxian, Deng Fa, Zhang Wentian, Yang Shangkun, Peng Zhen, Gao Gang and Ye Jianying attended one of the most important meetings in CCP history: the Politburo promoted Mao to its chairman (Liao Gailong 1991: 444). At the same time a new Secretariat was formed and included only three members: Chairman Mao, Liu Shaoqi and Ren Bishi (ZK 1943: 599).

Eight years after the Zunyi Conference, Mao Zedong finally took over the leadership of the CCP. This was the most important change in the leadership since the Long March. Still, Chinese politicians and historians did not even give a name to that decisive Politburo meeting and Western scholars hardly noticed it. The text of the Politburo decision was kept secret for 40 years.

At the same time, the Politburo established new committees for propaganda and organisation, which were controlled by the Politburo and Secretariat. Mao Zedong, Wang Jiaxiang, Qin Bangxian and He Kequan became members of the Propaganda Committee, the secretary was Mao Zedong and his deputy Wang Jiaxiang. The Propaganda Committee supervised the CC Propaganda department, the CC newspaper *Liberation Daily*, Xinhua News Agency and the Central Party School. Liu Shaoqi, Wang Jiaxiang, Kang Sheng, Chen Yun, Zhang Wentian, Deng Fa, Yang Shangkun and Ren Bishi became members of the Organisation Committee, the secretary was Liu Shaoqi. The Organisation Committee supervised the CC Departments for Organisation and for United Front Work (Central Committee 1943: 598–599). (See Table 16)

This decision was, in many ways, remarkable. Only with his appointment to chairman of the Politburo and Secretariat, did Mao Zedong take over the Party leadership – more than seven years after the end of the Long March. The Politburo also agreed that, when there was disunity in the Secretariat, the chairman should decide. Major decisions still had to be made by the – unchanged – Politburo, where Mao did not have a majority.

Table 16: The Party leadership from 20 March 1943

Secretariat	Mao Zedong (Chairman), Liu Shaoqi, Ren Bishi
Propaganda committee	Mao Zedong (secretary), **Wang Jiaxiang (deputy secretary)**, **Qin Bangxian**, **He Kequan**
Organisation committee	Liu Shaoqi (secretary), **Wang Jiaxiang**, Kang Sheng, Chen Yun, **Zhang Wentian**, Deng Fa, **Yang Shangkun**, Ren Bishi

Note: '28 Bolsheviks' = **bold**
(Source: Central Committee 1943: 598–599)

In the new, smaller Secretariat, there was – for the first time in a decade – no 'Bolshevik' and their most important ally, Zhou Enlai, was missing, too. The appointment of the two other secretaries is also interesting. Liu Shaoqi and Ren Bishi had been early CCP members, but did not really play a leading role in the 1930s. Even though Ren had led the 1931 CC delegation to the Jiangxi Soviet, he lost influence with the arrival of Zhou Enlai in the following winter and was sent to another communist base on the border of Jiangxi and Hunan. He reached the Northwest at the end of 1936. From March 1938 he represented the CCP at the Comintern in Moscow. (Zhang Xuexin 1994: 247ff.) This stay was important in two ways. First, Ren Bishi and his predecessor, Wang Jiaxiang, presented Mao Zedong and his policies more positively than Wang Ming had done and contributed to the change of the attitude of the Comintern leadership regarding to Mao (Zhang Xuexin 1994: 422ff.). Second, when Ren Bishi returned to China in 1940, he was seen as a Comintern representative – as Wang Ming was seen in 1937 – which strengthened his position and weakened that of Wang Ming. Liu Shaoqi, who had been an early activist of the labour movement, had lost influence due to the rise of the 'Bolsheviks' and did not play an important role in the Soviet. After the arrival of the Red Army in the Northwest, he had left the First Army and in the following six years organised communist underground work in North and East China. He only returned to Yan'an at the end of 1942. As Ren and Liu had been Party members since the early 1920s and studied in Moscow before the 'Bolsheviks' did, they were well-known and respected. Because they were not close to Mao or the 'Bolsheviks', they were acceptable to most leading communists.

What is also impressing, is that all three members of the new Secretariat came from the Southern Province of Hunan. Thus the thirteen-year rule of Eastern Chinese (Zhou Enlai, Wang Ming, Wang Jiaxiang, Qin Bangxian, Zhang Wentian, Chen Yun and Kang Sheng) ended. The 'Bolsheviks' were strongly represented on both committees. There were no changes in the composition of the Politburo.

One interesting aspect of the timing of Mao Zedong's appointment to Politburo chairman is the fact that it happened just ten days after the publication of Chiang Kai-shek's book *China's Fate* (*Zhongguo zhi mingyun*), which was distributed in millions of copies and praised as a masterpiece of the KMT leader (Jaffe 1947: 18). At that, time there were considerations within the CCP leadership, that the communists also needed a leading personality, with a high profile in the media, to present an alternative to the KMT.

Figure 11: Mao Zedong and Chen Yun in Yan'an.

The appointment of Mao was, however, not – as sometimes was assumed (Wylie 1980: 205) – a reaction to the dissolution of the Communist International. That only happened two months after the Politburo meeting.

The Proclamation of 'Mao Zedong Thought'

On 8 July 1943, less than four months after the promotion of Mao, the *Liberation Daily* published an article by Wang Jiaxiang, in which, for the first time, the term 'Mao Zedong Thought' (*Mao Zedong sixiang*) was propagated (Wang Jiaxiang xuanji bianjizu 1989: 340–360). This was a contribution to the twenty-second anniversary of the founding of the CCP and the sixth anniversary of the beginning of the Anti-Japanese War. In a CC circular of 8 August this article was declared obligatory reading for Party cadres (Kampen 1989b: 720–722).

In the following months, preparations for the publication of the first edition of the *Selected Works of Mao Zedong's* (*Mao Zedong Xuanji*) were started. The five-volume edition appeared in the summer of 1944.

THE SECOND CONTROVERSY OVER CCP HISTORY

A few months after Mao's appointment to the leadership and the official proclamation of his 'Thought', the Politburo started a new discussion on the history of the CCP in the 1930s. This controversy was longer and more intensive than the one in 1941, it started in September and ended in December 1943. Zhou Enlai had been recalled from Chongqing and could no longer avoid criticism. While Zhou and Zhang Wentian were willing to criticise their earlier activities, Qin Bangxian did not co-operate.

On 28 December, the Secretariat passed a directive in which Wang Ming and Qin Bangxian were explicitly criticised (Jin Chongji 1989: 553–563; Cao Zhongbin 1991: 455).
But even after the dissolution of the Comintern Zhou Enlai and Wang Ming received support from Moscow: on 22 December 1943 Dimitrov wrote to Mao and indicated opposition to the expulsion of Wang Ming and Zhou Enlai from the CCP and to criticism of their earlier activities (Zhou Guoquan 1990: 440–418; Cao Zhongbin 1991: 455). This not only shows, that even in 1943 Moscow exerted influence on the CCP, but also indicates, that their expulsion was planned or, at least, considered likely.

THE SEVENTH PLENUM AND THE *RESOLUTION ON PARTY HISTORY*

On 21 May 1944 the Seventh Plenum of the Sixth Central Committee started in Yan'an. More than five years had passed since the

Figure 12: Mao Zedong and his secretary Hu Qiaomu.

Sixth Plenum, when the early opening of the next Party congress was planned and announced. This Plenum was quite unusual. It consisted of several meetings that lasted until 20 April 1945, that is, for eleven months. In the first session seventeen CC members participated: Mao Zedong, Zhu De, Liu Shaoqi, Ren Bishi, Zhou Enlai, Kang Sheng, Peng Dehuai, Zhang Wentian, Deng Fa, Chen Yun, Qin Bangxian, Li Weihan, Li Fuchun, Wu Yuzhang, Yang Shangkun, Kong Yuan and Chen Yu. Fourteen other communists were present. Among the Politburo members, Wang Ming and Wang

Jiaxiang were absent; both were – officially – ill. On 21 May, the first day, an important decision was made: Mao Zedong was appointed chairman of the Central Committee and of the presidium of the Plenum. In addition to Mao, the Presidium included Zhu De, Liu Shaoqi, Ren Bishi and Zhou Enlai. It was also decided that during the Plenum the Politburo and Secretariat would not meet; the Presidium took over their responsibilities (Liao Gailong 1991: 451). This meant that the Politburo, which still included the 'Bolsheviks' Wang Ming, Qin Bangxian, Zhang Wentian and Wang Jiaxiang, was deprived of power, without being dissolved or reorganised. It was also remarkable that the five-member Presidium did not include any of the 'Bolsheviks' who had been represented in the Party leadership for thirteen years (since 1931). In fact, only Zhu De and Zhou Enlai were added to the Secretariat of 1943 (Mao Zedong, Liu Shaoqi and Ren Bishi). Ren Bishi and Zhou Enlai were former allies of the 'Bolsheviks'. The reappointment of Zhou indicates that his repeated self-criticisms were considered convincing and sufficient. It might also be argued that the inclusion of Zhu and Zhou in the Presidium had more symbolic and practical purposes and did not represent a shift in the balance of power. Due to their earlier contacts with the Kuomintang, both played an important role in united front work; Zhu was also the only representative of the Army and quite popular; Zhou had a lot of experience with foreign diplomats and journalists.

The 'Resolution on some questions in the history of Our Party'

One of the most important documents in and on the history of the CCP is the *Resolution on some questions in the history of Our Party*. After its publication in the 1950s, this resolution was also translated into several Western languages but was, for several reasons, often misinterpreted or misunderstood.

1. The publication of the resolution as an appendix to one of Mao's speeches in the third volume of his *Selected Works* (in 1953) led to the conclusion that Mao was the author and it was described as Mao's 'interpretation' (Dorrill 1974: 63) and 'version' (Wylie 1980: 263) of CCP history, and 'Mao's resolution' (Saich 1995: 299). It was, however, a collective publication, which was first drafted by Wang Jiaxiang, and revised by Mao Zedong, Ren Bishi, Zhang Wentian and other Politburo

members. The aim of its creation, was mainly to achieve consensus among numerous leading Party members. Feng Hui (1986) and Hu Qiaomu (1994) have recently described the complicated history of the resolution and its numerous re-writings in considerable detail (see Kampen 1989b: 716–722). But even without this insider knowledge, a close look at the version printed in Mao's *Selected Works* indicates that it is not very 'Maoist'. First, Chen Shaoyu (Wang Ming) is mentioned and criticised just about half a dozen times, but Li Lisan and the 'Li Lisan-line', more than twenty times. It is not very likely that Mao was very interested in criticising his enemies' enemy. On the other hand, people like Ren Bishi, Wang Jiaxiang, Zhang Wentian and Zhou Enlai were very interested in claiming that – even though they may have been wrong after 1931 – they were at least right in 1930 and 1931 (in fighting Li Lisan). Second, while the struggles in Shanghai of 1930 (which did not involve Mao) are discussed in considerable detail, negative events from Mao's point of view – the Ningdu Conference, the struggle against the 'Luo Ming line', the Fifth Plenum, the failure to defend the Jiangxi Soviet and the disastrous beginning of the Long March – are only mentioned briefly and there are hardly any details indicating who was responsible. Third, the Resolution concentrates on the period before the Long March, when Mao had no contact or conflict with Wang Ming. The period when they really clashed (in 1937 and 1938) is not covered at all. Fourth, if this document is one person's view of CCP history and he is regarded as an undisputed leader, why should there have been four years of endless discussions among Politburo members?

2. The text was printed as an appendix to a speech by Mao of April 1944, but was only passed 'in principle' in April 1945. Not only is the gap of twelve months important, but also the fact that the text, which was based on a draft made in the autumn of 1941, was repeatedly discussed and revised. The passing 'in principle' in April 1945 was closely connected to the opening of the Seventh Party Congress and the election of a new Central Committee and Politburo. Originally the *Resolution on some questions in the history of Our Party* was planned to be presented to the Party congress, but to avoid controversial discussions it was

only passed by the Central Committee. Officially, the *Resolution on some questions in the history of Our Party* was passed in August 1945 by the Central Committee.

3. The 1945 versions of the *Resolution on some questions in the history of Our Party* are hardly known. All Western authors who have claimed to analyse and quote from the '1945 resolution' (Hsiao 1961; Harrison 1972; Dorrill 1974; Wylie 1980; Saich 1995) have indeed only had access to the version published in 1953. Until the publication in the third volume of Mao's *Selected Works* in 1953, it was repeatedly revised. But between 1945 and 1953 conditions had completely changed, the Civil War had started and ended, the People's Republic was founded with Mao Zedong as head of state and Zhou Enlai as prime minister, Qin Bangxian and Stalin had died, and the CCP had – in 1950 – passed another decision on Wang Ming; in the same year Wang left for Moscow. Important information on the revisions can be found in the memoirs of Hu Qiaomu, who had been Mao's secretary for several years and who participated in the revisions. According to Hu Qiaomu, in 1945 Wang Ming and Qin Bangxian were not explicitly mentioned as the representatives of the 'incorrect' left line in the early 1930s. The names were only added in the early 1950s. Between 1945 and 1953 many references to Mao Zedong and 'Mao Zedong Thought' were changed, added or deleted (Hu Qiaomu 1994: 305–330).

The explicit mentioning of the names of the communists responsible for the 'incorrect' policies of the 1930s was less important for Mao than for the other people involved. It was obvious that Mao had been the victim of their activities and was not responsible for the errors and failures of that period. More difficult was the situation for those 'Bolsheviks', who had distanced themselves from Wang Ming and Qin Bangxian (Wang Jiaxiang, Zhang Wentian) and for the 'early allies' (Zhou Enlai, Ren Bishi, Chen Yun, Kang Sheng), who had co-operated with Wang and Qin. These communists participated in the drafting of the *Resolution* and were very interested in preventing the appearance of their names in connection with Wang and Qin. By repeated pledges of loyalty towards Mao and several self criticisms, the six people mentioned succeeded in this aim.

Figures 13 and 14: Participants of the CCP's Seventh Congress (1945).

THE SEVENTH PARTY CONGRESS AND THE ELECTION OF A NEW CCP LEADERSHIP

The Seventh Congress of the Chinese Communist Party started on 23 April in Yan'an and ended on 11 June 1945. Official delegates numbered 547 and 208 other participants took part and represented 1.2 million Party members (Ma Qibin 1991: 691). This CCP congress was very important. It was the first Party congress for seventeen years. In contrast to the Sixth Party congress of 1928 which had been held in Moscow (because in China there was no safe meeting place), in 1945 Yan'an was the centre of a large powerful communist base with millions of inhabitants.

On 9 June, a new Central Committee was elected and included 44 members. Even though everything was carefully planned, the result was surprising and this led to an unusual reaction by Mao Zedong. On 10 June he gave a short speech and declared that Wang Jiaxiang had not been elected a CC member. Mao praised Wang's contributions and asked the delegates to elect him as alternate member. On the same day 33 alternate members were elected and Wang Jiaxiang gained the second highest number of votes (Mao Zedong 1945: 32–33).

On 19 June the new Central Committee met for the first time and promoted 13 members to the Politburo, five also entered the Secretariat (Ma Qibin 1991: 691). (See Table 17)

Table 17: The Party leadership after the Seventh CCP Congress

Chairman of CC, Politburo and Secretariat	Mao Zedong
Secretariat	Mao Zedong, Zhu De, Liu Shaoqi, Zhou Enlai, Ren Bishi
Politburo	Mao Zedong, Zhu De, Zhou Enlai, Liu Shaoqi, Ren Bishi, Chen Yun, Kang Sheng, Gao Gang, Peng Zhen, Dong Biwu, Lin Boqu, **Zhang Wentian**, Peng Dehuai

Note: '28 Bolsheviks' = **bold**
(Source: Ma Qibin 1991: 691)

Even though the Seventh Party Congress was a triumph for Mao, the newly elected Politburo was not dominated by his supporters and should not be called 'Maoist leadership' (Teiwes 1995: 339).

Mao did not have a majority. Even Zhu De and Peng Dehuai, who were probably closest to him, had worked together with Qin Bangxian, Zhou Enlai and Zhang Guotao. Zhu De, who was often regarded as Mao's loyal supporter, had known Zhou much earlier and was, in fact, introduced to the CCP by Zhou. Mao's strength lay in the errors and mistakes of the highest ranking members of the Politburo and their vulnerability. Most of them (Zhou Enlai, Ren Bishi, Chen Yun, Kang Sheng, Dong Biwu, Zhang Wentian) had closely co-operated with Wang Ming and Qin Bangxian, Zhu De with Zhang Guotao.

The five-member Secretariat of 1945 which was identical with the Presidium elected in 1944, was relatively stable. Even though there were contradictions and differences of opinion, the co-operation of Mao Zedong, Liu Shaoqi, Zhou Enlai and Zhu De worked for twenty years – until the outbreak of the Cultural Revolution. Ren Bishi died in 1950 and was replaced by Chen Yun, who had first entered the Secretariat in 1934.

SUMMARY

The analysis of the struggles within the CCP leadership in the late 1930s and early 1940s shows that Mao Zedong only became Party leader in 1943 and not in 1935 or 1938. In addition to external factors, such as the South-Anhui Incident (1941) and the dissolution of the Comintern (1943) the most important factor in Mao's rise was not his own strength, but the change in the attitude of former allies of the '28 Bolsheviks', i.e. Ren Bishi, Zhou Enlai, Chen Yun, Kang Sheng. There was also a growing influence of Party leaders from North China like Gao Gang and Peng Zhen, who were not active supporters of Mao, but who – like Liu Shaoqi – opposed Wang Ming and Qin Bangxian.

Wang Ming has often been described as Mao's main opponent during the Rectification Movement. But as Wang claimed illness in October 1941 and withdrew from active work in the Politburo, he played only a secondary role. Two of his major allies, however, were still active and powerful: Qin Bangxian, who was responsible for propaganda in Yan'an, and Zhou Enlai, who led united front work in Chongqing.

Figure 15: A Chinese delegation in Moscow (1951). *From right*: Stalin, Zhou Enlai, Li Fuchun, Zhang Wentian.

In this context it is important to realise that the criticism aimed at the '28 Bolsheviks' and their allies covered two different phases: the 'leftist' years (1931–35) and the 'rightist' years (1937–38). Wang Ming did not play an important role in the first phase; before the Long March there was no direct confrontation between Mao and Wang. Mao did not leave the Jiangxi Soviet and Wang never entered it. Wang Ming's publications and activities in Moscow did not indicate that he saw Mao as a major opponent or rival. On the one hand, Wang was never particularly interested in Mao's activities concerning the peasant movement; on the other hand, Wang regarded Li Lisan and the 'Trotskyites' as his main enemies.

In contrast, Mao's conflicts with Zhou Enlai and Qin Bangxian had tremendous political and personal consequences. It should be remembered that the campaigns organised by Zhou and Qin (criticising the 'Luo Ming–line') affected Mao, his supporters and his own brother, Mao Zetan. Zhou and Qin also decided that many of Mao's supporters should stay in Jiangxi and not join the Long March. Mao Zetan and many other supporters of Mao were killed when KMT troops arrived.

In the early 1940s, Qin Bangxian was mainly criticised for 'leftist' strategies in the early 1930s, Wang Ming for 'rightist' strategies in the late 1930s, but only Zhou Enlai played a leading role in both phases. Thus, the combined criticism of 'leftist' and 'rightist' errors in the *Resolution on some questions in the history of Our Party* (Central Committee 1953) and Hu Qiaomu's *Thirty Years of the Communist Party of China* (1951) mainly affected Zhou Enlai. The main representative of the 'erroneous Wang Ming–line' was not Wang Ming but Zhou Enlai.

Conclusion

At the beginning of this study it was shown that the main elements of the story of the '28 Bolsheviks', which dominated Western scholarship for half a century, are contradicted by the Chinese sources published since 1979. In the spring of 1930, the Comintern did not send a homogeneous group of Chinese students – together with Pavel Mif – to China to overthrow the CCP leadership led by Li Lisan. Biographical sources recently published in the People's Republic of China show, that the 28 persons involved differed considerably in their geographical and social origins, age, education and political experience. They did not travel to Moscow together, did not return together and did not have much influence in the Party leadership. To push through its policies, the Comintern sent Politburo members Zhou Enlai and Qu Qiubai to China, recalled Li Lisan to Moscow and removed him from the Party leadership without involvement by the '28 Bolsheviks'.

It was also shown that the '28 Bolsheviks' did not organise a *putsch* to take over the leadership at the Fourth Plenum in January 1931. Only a few 'Bolsheviks' participated in the Plenum and very few were elected to the Party leadership. The acceptance of the Comintern line at the Plenum was mainly due to the participation of its representative, Pavel Mif, and not to efforts by the 'Bolsheviks'. Mif depended on the support of experienced and respected functionaries, particularly on Zhou Enlai. The influence of the 'Bolsheviks' in the CCP leadership only increased slowly and this was a result of the arrests of the CCP leaders He Mengxiong, Gu Shunzhang and Xiang Zhongfa, as well as the transfer of Zhang Guotao, Ren Bishi and Zhou Enlai to different communist bases. When Qin Bangxian

Figure 16: Mao Zedong and Hu Qiaomu (*second from left*) in Moscow (1957).

ook over in the autumn of 1931 the provisional leadership had little nfluence outside the city of Shanghai. Together with Qin Bangxian, Chen Yun and Kang Sheng also entered the top leadership.

It was then revealed, that the story of the transfer of many or all Bolsheviks' to the Central Soviet and the ousting of Mao Zedong by he 'Bolsheviks' is not true. Only a few 'Bolsheviks' entered the Central Soviet and the confrontation between these 'Bolsheviks' and Mao had no immediate consequences. With the arrival of Xiang Ying, Ren Bishi and Zhou Enlai in 1931 and 1932, Mao was already deprived of power. Leading 'Bolsheviks' such as Qin Bangxian and Zhang Wentian only arrived in 1933.

The well-known 'fall' of the 'Bolsheviks' during the Long March did not take place. Qin Bangxian handed the post of 'general secretary' o Zhang Wentian, who belonged to the same group. Mao Zedong became just a member of the Standing Committee of the Politburo, but did not rise to formal or *de facto* leader of the Party. The position of Politburo or Central Committee chairman often attributed to him did not exist in the 1930s. Zhou Enlai and Zhu De did not lose their leading posts in the army hierarchy, but Mao gradually increased his influence in the military leadership. He was first supported by the 'Bolsheviks' Wang Jiaxiang and Zhang Wentian, but the change of mind of Zhou Enlai was decisive. However, Zhou and several military leaders mainly opposed Otto Braun's strategies, they were not fervent supporters of Mao Zedong.

In the three years following the Long March, Mao was often in a minority position: he was unable to push through his ideas of a united front and was defeated in the controversy following the Xi'an Incident. When Wang Ming returned to China, he was immediately supported by Zhou Enlai and other Party leaders, who had previously supported Mao. These examples also prove, that the Comintern had not lost influence. The Comintern made the restoration of communication links possible, propagated its united front policy and achieved the release of Chiang Kai-shek in Xi'an. Just because of the strength of Comintern influence, its withdrawal of support for Wang Ming in 1938 was so important.

It was only in 1943 that Mao Zedong became chairman of the Politburo and Secretariat and, thus, leader of the CCP. There are no convincing sources indicating an earlier *de facto* leadership before this date. Until 1943 the CCP had a collective leadership. Mao's promotion to the leadership was supported by Ren Bishi and Kang Sheng, who had earlier worked with the 'Bolsheviks', and Liu Shaoqi and Wang Jiaxiang. Soon after Mao's appointment his position was further strengthened by the propagation of 'Mao Zedong Thought' (1943) the publication of his *Selected Works* (1944) and the election to CC chairman (1945). But even after 1945 Mao and his supporters had no majority in the Politburo.

The well-known claims of Western scholars quoted in Chapter I regarding the return of the '28 Bolsheviks' with Pavel Mif, the take over at the Fourth Plenum and the confrontation with Mao and regarding the fall of the '28 Bolsheviks' and takeover of Mao Zedong at the Zunyi Conference have all been proved wrong. This also shows that the above-mentioned 'two-line model' is untenable. From 1931 to 1935 there was no rule of the '28 Bolsheviks' and after 1935 there was no unchallenged leadership of Mao Zedong. Similarly there was no permanent loss of power by the Comintern. After the

Long March, the Comintern actively propagated and pushed through its united front policy.

Instead, the analysis of the evolution of the Party leadership between 1931 and 1945 has demonstrated the decisive role of other politicians. Xiang Ying, Ren Bishi, Liu Shaoqi, Kang Sheng and Chen Yun played an important role in certain periods; Zhou Enlai dominated throughout these years and co-operated with Li Lisan, Wang Ming and Qin Bangxian; after all of them had failed, Zhou supported Mao Zedong. Major reasons for his political survival were his unusual flexibility and ability to present convincing self criticisms; in addition, he had superior competence in political, military and organisational matters. Most of the '28 Bolsheviks' just concentrated on ideology and propaganda, and failed.

In the accounts of CCP history in Hu Qiaomu's *Thirty Years of the Communist Party of China* of 1951 and in the *Resolution on some questions in the history of Our Party* of 1953 (the only available version) the following points are important:

> The definition, that the supporters of the 'third erroneous "Left" line' were the rulers between 1931 and 1935 and the main opponents of Mao Zedong.
>
> The explicit naming of Wang Ming and Qin Bangxian as the persons mainly responsible while not mentioning Zhou Enlai.
>
> The link up of two 'erroneous' lines before and after the Long March: 'Some comrades represented by Wang Ming who had committed serious "Left" errors during the period of the Second Revolutionary Civil War now [1937] criticised and opposed the Party line from a Right-opportunist standpoint.' (Hu 1951: III/16)

The last aspect is particularly important. A study of CCP documents shows that, before his return in November 1937, Wang Ming was not identified with the 'Left' deviation of 1931–35 and was not held responsible. Only after the 'Right' deviation of 1937–38, the earlier 'Left' deviation was criticised and identified with him. Looking at the three main 'victims' of the rectification movement, Wang Ming, Zhou Enlai and Qin Bangxian, it is obvious, that Qin Bangxian played a decisive role between 1931 and 1935 and Wang Ming between 1937 and 1938, but only Zhou Enlai was a top leader in both phases and, thus, the above-mentioned link up mainly related to him. Considering this aspect, it is remarkable, that in the above-mentioned

Figure 17: Wang Jiaxiang, Zhang Wentian (*middle*) and Zhou Enlai at the Geneva Conference (1954).

texts only Wang and Qin are mentioned explicitly, while Zhou Enlai was spared. However, Zhou was only spared as a result of repeated self-critical confessions in the Politburo, at the Seventh Plenum and the Seventh Party congress (1943–45) and following the notification of Party congress participants about his role. As his 'errors' were known to the higher levels of the Party, he could always be attacked and dismissed. Thus, in contrast to Liu Shaoqi, who had a 'clean' past, Zhou Enlai could be used for decades at the top of the Party and government, without posing a serious threat to Mao Zedong.

The development of the CCP leadership until the Seventh Party congress and the re-election of the Politburo also shows that the new leadership was not dominated by supporters of Mao, but included several small groups and individuals: Liu Shaoqi, who had worked in North China, and rising Northern Chinese communists (Peng Zhen, Gao Gang), army commanders (Zhu De, Peng Dehuai) as well as 'Bolsheviks' and their former 'allies' (Zhang Wentian, Zhou Enlai, Kang Sheng, Chen Yun, Ren Bishi, Dong Biwu) and Lin Boqu. This shows that the 'allies' were the largest group; in the long term they were also the most successful. For many decades, Zhou Enlai, Kang Sheng and Chen Yun played a leading role in PRC politics. However, the balance of power of 1945 was not stable. The purges of Gao Gang (1954), Peng Dehuai and Zhang Wentian (1959) as well as Liu Shaoqi and Peng Zhen (1966) suggest that the small groups continuously fought each other. Surprisingly, the most important victims, who often died in mysterious circumstances, were communists who had – at different times – been very close to Mao (Gao Gang, Peng Dehuai, Liu Shaoqi and Lin Biao). On the other hand, the 'allies' Zhou Enlai, Kang Sheng, Chen Yun and Dong Biwu reached an impressive age and were in power until their death. This again demonstrates that there was no 'two-line struggle' after 1949.

The conclusions and assumptions presented above are based mainly on Chinese sources, but cannot be found in PRC publications. The term '28 Bolsheviks', which was often used in the West and in Taiwan, has not been used in official publications in the People's Republic. In the 1950s, when China and the Soviet Union were allies and former 'Bolsheviks' occupied leading positions in the Party and government, the term was proscribed. During the Cultural Revolution the story of the 'Bolsheviks' appeared mainly in unofficial publications and wall-posters, particularly in connection with the

Figure 18: Zhou Enlai (*left*), Zhang Wentian and Wang Jiaxiang (*third and fourth seated*) at the Geneva Conference (1954).

criticism of 'pro-Soviet' activities of Yang Shangkun, Zhang Wentian and Wang Jiaxiang. In the 1970s and 1980s, when 'Bolsheviks' critic ised in the Cultural Revolution were rehabilitated and when Yang Shangkun, the most prominent survivor and friend of Deng Xiaoping became head of state, Party historians still avoided that term. In the official publications on the 1930s, usually Wang Ming and Qin Bangxian and 'representatives' and 'supporters' of the 'Wang Ming Line' are mentioned without providing many names. The main reason behind the strict control of related publications seems to be that the

Figure 19: The CCP leadership in the 1950s. *From left*: Zhu De, Zhou Enlai, Chen Yun, Liu Shaoqi, Mao Zedong and Deng Xiaoping.

most important politician of that period, Zhou Enlai, who closely co-operated with the 'Bolsheviks', should not be publicly criticised. Because there has been considerable criticism of Mao's policies and private life, Zhou seems to be even more important as a political and moral model.

The Zunyi Conference is a difficult and important problem. In the 1981 *Resolution* it was again described as a turning point in Chinese history and in 1985 the fiftieth anniversary received enormous attention. This did not mean, that a detailed description of the events of 1935 was provided. Numerous documents and memoirs were published, but they were carefully selected and edited to maximise the propaganda value of the conference and to avoid provoking contradictions. The Long March in general and the Zunyi Conference in particular, were described as turning points in the modern Chinese history, the Chinese revolution, the history of the Party and in Mao's rise. The 'success' of the conference is seen as the first step in defeating Japan and the KMT and the 'liberation' of China. Leading communists of the early 1980s such as Deng Xiaoping, Chen Yun, Yang Shangkun and Nie Rongzhen proudly emphasised their participation in this 'decisive' event.

From the perspective of the Chinese leadership, an official switch of Mao's takeover from 1935 to 1943 would only have disadvantages. It would cut his 'rule' by eight years and make his rise less glorious. Second, a long period in Party history without a strong leader might make a bad impression and create 'confusion'. In addition, it would also be difficult to hide the identity of Mao's opponents: Wang Ming and Zhou Enlai. Therefore a revision of the interpretation given in the two *Resolutions* is not very likely. As a consequence, it also seems unlikely that important sources, such as the document collection *Since the Sixth Party congress* or the original version of the *Resolution on some questions in the history of Our Party* will be published in the near future.

It is easy to understand the likely Chinese reasons for dealing with the rise of Mao and the Zunyi Conference, but it is very difficult to comprehend the reasons for the biased and misleading accounts of CCP history by numerous Western scholars.

More or less by coincidence, Edgar Snow played an important role in emphasising an early takeover by Mao. If Snow had not visited Bao'an in the summer of 1936 but Ruijin in 1934 or Yan'an in 1938, he would have talked to other politicians and would have got a different impression. He did, however, arrive shortly after the end of the First Army's Long March and before the arrival of Zhang Guotao (autumn 1936), Wang Ming (autumn 1937) and others. Snow thus met Mao Zedong when most Politburo members (Chen Yun, Kang Sheng, Liu Shaoqi, Wang Ming, Xiang Ying, Zhang Guotao and Zhu De) were absent. Just because Snow got the impression that Mao's position was very strong and publicised this view all over the world (including Moscow), he strengthened Mao's position. Snow was, however, rarely quoted in the anti-communist accounts of the 1950s; he had not written about the '28 Bolsheviks' and the Zunyi Conference.

Concerning the return of the 'Bolsheviks' in the spring of 1930, the alleged confrontation of Mao with the 'Bolsheviks' in Jiangxi and the appointment of Mao to Party chairman in Zunyi, there have never been reliable and convincing documents. In the 1950s, when the source material available was very limited, many scholars trusted a few and unreliable accounts, particularly *Red Stage* by Li Ang, who did not take part in the most important events of the 1930s. In the 1960s, KMT accounts, particularly the books by Warren Kuo and Hsiao Tso-liang, were widely used as they were published in English. In these publications the Soviet and Comintern influence was always

126

emphasised; the CCP was not just described as a political opponent in China, but as a representative of a foreign power; thus the 'patriotic' extermination policy of the KMT was legitimised. During the Cultural Revolution, the Red Guards highlighted the 'confrontation' between Mao and the 'Bolsheviks' and this again influenced Western studies. Simultaneously, Soviet (and East German) publications – Braun's *Comintern Agent* and Vladimirov's *Diaries*, which were also distributed in several Western languages – emphasised the conflict between the 'correct' Comintern line and the 'Maoist deviation'.

During the Cold War, when there was the idea of a big socialist camp from East Germany to East Asia, and during the Sino–Soviet conflict many politicians and scholars were interested in the relations between Mao and Stalin and between the Chinese CCP, the CPSU and the Comintern. During the Cultural Revolution the conflict between Mao and Liu Shaoqi inspired scholarly research. In both cases historical studies were undertaken to explain current problems. There was some research on the 'Bolsheviks' and Liu Shaoqi, but the role of other politicians who had died earlier or did not play a role in the Cultural Revolution (Xiang Ying, Ren Bishi, Deng Fa and Chen Yun) was neglected.

Obviously, the Cold War and the Sino–Soviet conflict provoked research on changes in the CCP leadership and the rise of Mao Zedong, but the results are not very useful. It is quite alarming that models, like the above-mentioned 'two-line model' (referring to the development of the CCP leadership between 1931 and 1945), which were based on very weak sources, survived for several decades without change despite the fact that there were substantial quantitative and qualitative improvements in the sources available.

Bibliography

Apter, David E. (1995), 'Discourse as power: Yan'an and the Chinese Revolution', in Tony Saich and Hans van de Ven (eds), *New Perspectives on the Chinese Communist Revolution*. Armonk, pp. 193–234.

Bachman, David (1985), *Chen Yun and the Chinese Political System*. Berkeley.

Bartke, Wolfgang (1981), *Who's Who in the People's Republic of China*. Armonk.

—— (1985), *Die großen Chinesen der Gegenwart*. Frankfurt.

Benton, Gregor (1975), 'The "Second Wang Ming Line" (1935–38)'. *The China Quarterly*. no. 61, pp. 61–94.

Boorman, Howard L. (1967), *Biographical Dictionary of Republican China*. New York.

Brandt, Conrad (1952), *A Documentary History of Chinese Communism*. Cambridge (Mass.).

—— (1958), *Stalin's Failure in China*. Cambridge (Mass.).

Braun, Otto (1973), *Chinesische Aufzeichnungen*. Berlin.

—— (1982) *A Comintern Agent in China*. London.

Cao Runfang & Pan Xianying (1984), *Zhongguo gongchandang jiguan fazhanshi* [The development of the organization of the Chinese Communist Party], Beijing.

Cao Zhongbin (1989), *Letter to the Author*.

Cao Zhongbin & Dai Maolin (1988), *Mosike Zhongshan Daxue yu Wang Ming* [Moscow's Sun Yat-sen University and Wang Ming], Harbin.

—— (1991), *Wang Ming zhuan* [A biography of Wang Ming], Changchun.

Central Committee (1943), 'Zhongyang guanyu Zhongyang jigou tiaozheng ji jingjian de jueding' [The Central Committee's decision on the adjustment and simplification of the central organs], in: *Zhonggong zhongyang qingnian yundong wenjian xuanbian*, Beijing, 1988, 597–603.

Central Committee (1953), 'Resolution on some questions in the history of our party', in Mao Tse-tung, *Selected Works of Mao Tse-tung*. 1956, Vol. 1, pp. 171ff.

Chang, Kuo-t'ao (1972), *The Rise of the Chinese Communist Party 1928–1938*. Lawrence.

Ch'en, Jerome (1967), *Mao and the Chinese Revolution*. London.

—— (1969), 'Resolutions of the Tsunyi Conference'. *The China Quarterly*. No. 40, pp. 1–38.

—— (1986), 'The Communist Movement 1927–1937'. *Cambridge History of China*. Vol. 13, pp. 168–229.

Chen Lifu (1987), 'Chen Lifu guanyu canjia Kangzhan zhunbei gongzuo zhi huiyi' [Chen Lifu's memories concerning his participation in the preparations for the Anti-Japanese War]. *Dangshi ziliao tongxun*, 5–6, pp. 93–96.

Chen Rongfu (1990), *Dangdai Zhongguo shehuikexue xuezhe da cidian* [A dictionary of contemporary Chinese social scientists], Hangzhou.

Chen Xianqiang (1985), 'Shanghai – Ruijin mimi jiaotongxian gai-shu' [A description of the secret communication links between Shanghai and Ruijin]. *Dangshi ziliao congkan*, 4, 56–62.

Chen Xiuliang (1983), 'Mosike Zhongshan Daxue li de douzheng' [The struggle in Moscow's Sun Yat-sen University]. *Geming huiyilu zengkan*, 1, 44–67

Chen Yutang (1993), *Zhongguo jinxiandai renwu minghao da cidian* [A dictionary of pseudonyms of personalities in modern China], Hangzhou.

Cheng Zhongyuan (1993), *Zhang Wentian zhuan* [A biography of Zhang Wentian], Beijing.

Chesneaux, Jean (1977), *China From the 1911 Revolution to Liberation*. New York.

Clubb, O. E. (1971), *China and Russia*. New York.

Compton, Boyd (1952), *Mao's China, Party Reform Documents 1942–44*. Seattle.

Dittmar, Peter (1975), *Wörterbuch der chinesischen Revolution*. Freiburg.

Domes, Jürgen (1985), *Peng Te-huai – The Man and the Image*. Stanford.

Donovan, Peter (1981), *The Red Army in Kiangsi 1931–1934*. Ithaca.

Dorrill, William F. (1968), 'Transfer of legitimacy in the Chinese Communist Party: Origins of the Maoist myth'. *The China Quarterly*, no. 36, pp. 45–60.

—— (1974), 'Rewriting history to further Maoism: The Ningtu Conference of 1932', in James C. Hsiung (ed.), *The Logic of Maoism*. New York, pp. 62–85.

Dressler, Bernhard (1990), *Zur 'Sinisierung' des Marxismus*. Frankfurt.

Dreyer, June Teufel (1993), *China's Political System – Modernization and Tradition*. Houndmills.

Fairbank, John K. (1986), *The Great Chinese Revolution, 1900–1985*. New York.

Fang Xiao (1991), *Zhonggong dangshi bianyilu* [Controversies in CCP history], Taiyuan.

Fundamental Laws of the Chinese Soviet Republic (1934). London.

Feng Hui (1986), 'Mao Zedong lingdao qicao "Guanyu ruogan lishi wenti de jueyi" de jingguo' [How Mao Zedong led the drafting of the 'Resolution on certain historical questions']. *Wenxian he yanjiu*, 2, 10–16.

Garver, John (1988), *Chinese–Soviet Relations 1937–45*. New York.

—— (1988a), 'The origins of the Second United Front: the Comintern and the Chinese Communist Party'. *The China Quarterly*. no. 113, pp. 29–59.

Guillermaz, Jacques (1972), *A History of the Chinese Communist Party*. London.

Guo Zhiming (1987), 'Suqu zhongyangju de chengli' [The establishment of the Soviet's Central Bureau]. *Jiangxi dangshi tongxun*, 4, 2–5.

Harrison, James Pinckney (1972), *The Long March to Power – A History of the Chinese Communist Party*. London.

He Jinqing (1983), 'Yan'an zhengfeng yundong dashiji' [A chronology of the the Yan'an rectification movement], in: *Zhonggong dangshi ziliao*, 8, 313–358.

Heinzig, Dieter (1971), 'The Otto Braun memoirs and Mao's rise to Power'. *The China Quarterly*, no.46, pp. 274–288.

Hinz, Manfred (1973), *Räte–China – Dokumente der chinesischen Revolution (1927–1931)*. Frankfurt.

Hou, Fu-wu (1973), *A Short History of Chinese Communism*. Englewood Cliffs.

Hsiao, Tso-liang (1961), *Power Relations within the Chinese Communist Movement 1930–1934*. Seattle.

Hsü, Immanuel C. Y. (1995), *The Rise of Modern China*. New York.

Hsüeh Chün-tu (1960), *The Chinese Communist Movement*. Palo Alto.

Hu, Chi-hsi (1970), 'Hua Fu, the Fifth Encirclement and the Tsuny Conference'. *The China Quarterly*. no. 43, pp. 31–46.

—— (1980), 'Mao, Lin Biao and the Fifth Encirclement Campaign'. *The China Quarterly*. no. 82, pp. 250–280.

—— (1988), 'The Struggle for the Control of the Red Army in Jiangxi Mao vs. Zhou Enlai'. *Internationales Asienforum*. vol. 19, pp. 159–181

Hu Chiao-mu (1951), 'Thirty years of the Communist Party of China' *People's China*. vol. 4, nos 2–6.

—— (1959), *Thirty Years of the Communist Party of China*. Peking.

Hu Hua (1980ff.), *Zhonggong dangshi renwuzhuan* [Biographies of person alities in the history of the Chinese Communist Party], Xi'an.

Hu Qiaomu (1951), 'Zhongguo gongchandang de sanshinian' [Thirt years of the Communist Party of China]. *Xinhua Yuebao*, 7, 556–576

—— (1994), *Hu Qiaomu huiyi Mao Zedong* [Hu Qiaomu remember Mao Zedong], Beijing.

Hubei sheng Yingshan xianzhi bianzuan weiyuanhui (1990), *Yingsha xianzhi* [A gazetteer of Yingshan county], Wuhan.

Jaffe, Philip (1947), 'The secret of *China's Destiny*', in Chiang Kai-shek *China's Destiny*. London.

Jiang Huaxuan *et al.* (1991), *Zhongguo gongchandang huiyi gaiyao* [A de scription of conferences of the Chinese Communist Party] Shenyang.

Jin Chongji et al. (1989), *Zhou Enlai zhuan* [A biography of Zhou Enlai] Beijing.

Jue Shi (1988), 'Zhou Enlai yu Kangzhan chuqi de Changjiangju [Zhou Enlai and the Yangzi office at the beginning of the Anti Japanese War]. *Zhonggong dangshi yanjiu*, 2, 9–17.

Kagan, Richard C. (1974), 'The Comintern, the 28 Bolsheviks, and the alumni of Sun Yatsen-University'. *International Review of History and Political Science.* vol.11, no 1, pp. 79–90.

—— (1992), 'Long March', in Edwin Pak-wah Leung (ed.), *Historical Dictionary of Revolutionary China 1839–1976.* New York, pp. 236–238.

Kampen, Thomas (1986), 'The Zunyi Conference and the rise of Mao Zedong'. *Internationales Asienforum.* November 1986, pp. 347–360.

—— (1987), 'Changes in the leadership of the Chinese Communist Party during and after the Long March'. *Republican China.* 12, no.2, pp. 28–36.

—— (1989a), 'The Zunyi Conference and further steps in Mao's rise to power'. *The China Quarterly.* no.117, March, pp. 118–134.

—— (1989b), 'Wang Jiaxiang, Mao Zedong and the "Triumph of Mao Zedong Thought"'. *Modern Asian Studies.* October, pp. 705–727.

—— (1989c), 'From the December Conference to the Sixth Plenum: Wang Ming versus Mao Zedong'. *Republican China.* November, pp. 82–97.

—— (1990), 'Chinese translations of foreign publications on the history of the CCP and the People's Republic of China'. *CCP Research Newsletter.* Nos. 6 & 7, pp. 8–19.

—— (1993), 'The CCP's Central Committee Departments (1921–1991): A Study of Their Evolution'. *China Report.* pp. 299–317.

—— (1997), 'Deutsche und österreichische Kommunisten im revolutionären China'. *Jahrbuch für historische Kommunismus-forschung.* pp. 88–104.

Kataoka, Tetsuya (1974), *Resistance and Revolution in China.* Berkeley.

Kim, Ilpyong (1973), *The Politics of Chinese Communism.* Berkeley.

—— (1992), 'Tsunyi Conference', in Edwin Pak-wah Leung(ed.), *Historical Dictionary of Revolutionary China 1839–1976.* New York, pp. 434–435.

Klein, Donald and Anne Clark (1971), *Biographic Dictionary of Chinese Communism 1921–1965.* Cambridge (Mass.).

Kuo, Heng-yü (1975), *Maos Weg zur Macht und die Komintern.* Paderborn.

Kuo, Warren (1968), *Analytical History of Chinese Communist Party (Book Two).* Taipei.

—— (1970), *Analytical History of Chinese Communist Party (Book Three).* Taipei.

—— (1971), *Analytical History of Chinese Communist Party (Book Four)*. Taipei.

Ladany, Laszlo (1988), *The Communist Party of China and Marxism 1921–1985*. London.

Lawrance, Alan (1991), *Mao Zedong: A Bibliography*. Westport.

Lazitch, Branko and Milorad Drachkovitch (1986), *Biographical Dictionary of the Comintern*. Stanford.

Leung, Edwin Pak-wah (1992), *Historical Dictionary of Revolutionary China 1839–1976*. New York.

Levine, Marilyn (1992), 'Twenty-eight Bolsheviks' in Edwin Pak-wah Leung (ed.), *Historical Dictionary of Revolutionary China 1839–1976*. New York, pp. 439–441.

Li Ang (1942), *Hongse wutai* [Red stage], Chongqing.

Li Liangming (1993), *Xiang Ying pingzhuan* [A critical biography of Xiang Ying], Beijing.

Li Ping (1988), 'Chuli "Lisan wenti" shi de Zhou Enlai' [Zhou Enlai at the time when the 'Lisan problem' was solved]. *Zhonghua yinglie*, 2, 4–10.

Li Ping (1989), *Zhou Enlai nianpu* [A chronicle of Zhou Enlai], Beijing.

Li Weihan (1986), *Huiyi yu yanjiu* [Memories and studies], Beijing.

Li Yunlong (1987), 'Zhonggong zhongyang shujichu shi heshi sheli de?' [When was the CCP's central secretariat established?]. *Zhongyang dang'anguan congkan*, 5, 14–15.

Li Zhiguang (1983), 'Guanyu Zunyi Zhengzhiju kuodahuiyi ruogan qingkuang de diaocha baogao' [Investigation report on the circumstances of the enlarged politburo conference at Zunyi]. *Zhonggong dangshi ziliao*, 6, 16–34.

Li Zhiying (1994), *Bo Gu zhuan* [A biography of Bo Gu], Beijing.

Liao Gailong (1991), *Zhongguo gongchandang fazhan shidian* [The development of the Chinese Communist Party], Shenyang.

Liao Guoliang and Tian Yuanle (1987), *Zhongguo gongnong hongjun shijian renwu lu* [Events and personalities of the Chinese Workers' and Peasants' Red Army], Shanghai.

Litten, Freddy (1988), *Otto Brauns frühes Wirken in China*. München.

Liu Huafeng and Wang Yuting (1992), *Zhongguo gongchandang zuzhi gongzuo dashiji* [A chronicle of the organizational work of the Chinese Communist Party], Shenyang.

Liu Jintian (1992), *Lijie Zhongong zhongyang weiyuan renming cidian* [A dictionary of the members of the Central Committees of the CCP], Beijing.

Liu Mianyu (1991), 'Xiang Ying zai zhongyang suqu de gong yu guo' [Xiang Ying's achievements and errors in the Central Soviet]. *Jiangxi daxue xuebao: shekeban*, 1, 50–56.

Lötveit, Trygve (1979), *Chinese Communism 1931–1934*. London.

—— (1987), 'The Chinese Soviet Republic, 1931–1934', in: Yuming Shaw *Reform and Revolution in Twentieth Century China*. Taipei.

Luo Ming (1982), 'Guanyu "Luo Ming luxian wenti de huigu"' [A look back at the 'Luo Ming-line']. *Zhonggong dangshi ziliao*, 2, 234–270.

Lü Cheng (1991), *Dangde jianshe qishi nian jishi* [Seventy years of party construction], Beijing.

Ma Qibin (1991), *Zhongguo gongchandang chuangye sanshinian* [Thirty years of Chinese Communist Party construction], Beijing.

Mao Tse-tung (1936), 'Problems of Strategy in China's Revolutionary War', in *Selected Works of Mao Tse-tung*. Peking, 1967, Vol. 1, pp. 179–254.

—— (1937), 'The situation and tasks in the Anti-Japanese War after the fall of Shanghai and Taiyuan', in *Selected Works of Mao Tse-tung*. Peking, 1967, Vol. 2, pp. 61–74.

—— (1956), *Selected Works of Mao Tse-tung*. London.

—— (1966), 'Talk at the report meeting', in Stuart R. Schram, *Chairman Mao Talks to the People*. New York, 1974, pp. 264–269.

Mao Zedong (1941), 'Fandui zhuguanzhuyi he zongpaizhuyi' [Oppose subjectivism and sectarianism]. *Wenxian he yanjiu*, 1, 1985, 4–6.

—— (1945), 'Guanyu Wang Jiaxiang de pingjia' [An appraisal of Wang Jiaxiang]. *Wenxian he yanjiu*, 4, 1986, 32–33.

McLane, Charles B. (1958), *Soviet Policy and the Chinese Communists*. New York.

Miff, P. (1937), *China's Struggle for Freedom*. London.

Nie Rongzhen (1988), *Inside the Red Star*. Peking.

Nie Rongzhen (1984), *Nie Rongzhen huiyilu* [The memoirs of Nie Rongzhen], Beijing.

North, Robert C. (1968), *Chinese Communism*. New York.

—— (1963), *Moscow and Chinese Communists*. Stanford.

—— (1972), 'Communists of the Chinese Revolution', in Helen Foster Snow, *The Chinese Communists*. Westport.

Pang Xianzhi (1993), *Mao Zedong nianpu* [A chronicle of Mao Zedong] Beijing.

Payne, Robert (1965), *Mao Tse-tung*. Hamburg.

Price, Jane L. (1976), *Cadres, commanders and commissars*. Boulder.

Quanguo Zhonggong dangshi yanjiuhui (1987), *Kang-Ri minzu tongy zhanxian yu di'erci Guo-Gong hezuo* [The Anti-Japanese united from and the second cooperation of the Kuomintag and CCP], Beijing

Resolution on CPC History (1981), Beijing.

Rue, John E. (1966), *Mao Tse-tung in Opposition 1927–1935*. Stanford.

Saich, Tony (1995), 'Writing or Rewriting History? The Construction of the Maoist Resolution on Party History', in Tony Saich and Hans van de Ven (eds), *New Perspectives on the Chinese Communis Revolution*. Armonk, pp. 299–338.

Salisbury, Harrison (1985), *Long March*. New York.

Schram, Stuart (1967), *Mao Tse-tung*. Harmondsworth.

—— (1974), *Chairman Mao Talks to the People*. New York.

—— (1983), *Mao Zedong: A Preliminary Reassessment*. Hong Kong.

—— (1986), 'Mao Tse-tung's thought to 1949' in *Cambridge History o China*. Vol. 13, pp. 789–870.

—— (1995), *Mao's Road to Power, Vol. 3*. Armonk.

Schwartz, Benjamin I. (1951), *Chinese Communism and the Rise of Mao* Cambridge (Mass.).

Schwarz, Henry G. (1970), 'The Nature of Leadership: the Chinese Communists, 1930–1945'. *World Politics*. July, pp. 541–581.

Selden, Mark (1971), *The Yenan Way in Revolutionary China*. Cambridge (Mass.).

Seybolt, Peter (1986), 'Terror and conformity'. *Modern China*. vol. 12 no. 1, pp. 39–73.

Shanghai Municipal Police Files, Archive (Microfilm version).

Sheng, Michael (1992), 'Mao, Stalin and the formation of the Anti-Japanese United Front: 1935–37'. *The China Quarterly*. no. 129, pp. 151ff.

Sheng Ping (1991), *Zhongguo gongchandang renming da cidian* [A dictionary of personalities of the Chinese Communist Party], Beijing.

Sheng, Yueh (1971), *Sun Yat-sen University in Moscow and the Chinese Revolution – A Personal Account.* Kansas.

Shi Zhifu & Zhou Wenqi (1987), *Li De yu Zhongguo geming* [Otto Braun and the Chinese revolution], Beijing.

Shum, Kui-Kwong (1988), *The Chinese Communists' Road to Power – The Anti-Japanese National United Front (1935–1945).* Hong Kong.

Sima Lu (1979), 'Zhongong dangshi ji wenxian xuancui' [CCP history and selected documents]. *Zhanwang*, No. 425.

Snow, Edgar (1937), *Red Star over China.* London.

—— (1957), *Random Notes on Red China.* Cambridge (Mass.).

Snow, Helen Foster (1972), *The Chinese Communists.* Westport.

Stranahan, Patricia (1990), 'The last battle: Mao and the Internationalists' fight for the *Liberation Daily*', *The China Quarterly.* no. 123, pp. 522–537.

Suqu zhongyangju (1932), 'Suqu zhongyangju Ningdu huiyi jingguo jianbao' [A brief report on the Ningdu conference of the Soviet's Central Bureau], in Zhongguo renmin jiefangjun Guofang Daxue dangshi dangjian zhenggong jiaoyanshi, *Zhonggong dangshi jiaoxue cankao ziliao* [Teaching materials on the history of the CCP], 15, 1986, S. 176–177.

Swarup, Shanti (1966), *A Study of the Chinese Communist Movement.* Oxford.

Tang Chunliang (1989), *Li Lisan zhuan* [A biography of Li Lisan], Harbin.

Tarsitano, Frank (1979), *The Collapse of the Kiangsi Soviet and the Fifth Encirclement Campaign.* New York.

Teiwes, Frederick C. (1976), 'The origins of rectification'. *The China Quarterly.* no. 65, pp. 15–53.

—— (1995), 'From a Leninist to a charismatic Party: The CCP's changing leadership', in Tony Saich and Hans van de Ven (eds), *New Perspectives on the Chinese Communist Revolution.* Armonk, pp. 339–387.

Thornton, Richard C. (1969), *The Comintern and the Chinese Communists.* Seattle.

—— (1973), *China the Struggle for Power 1917–1972.* Bloomington.

—— (1982), *China – A Political History.* Boulder.

Titov, A. (1976), 'About the Tsunyi Conference'. *Far Eastern Affairs,* no. 1, pp. 99–110.

Uhalley, Stephen (1975), *Mao Tse-tung, A Critical Biography.* New York.

—— (1988) *A History of the Chinese Communist Party.* Stanford.

Van Slyke, Lyman (1986), 'The Chinese Communist Movement during the Sino-Japanese War 1937–1945', in *Cambridge History of China.* Vol. 13, Cambridge.

Vladimirov, Peter (1975), *The Vladimirov Diaries.* New York.

Waller, Derek (1973), *The Kiangsi Soviet Republic.* Berkeley.

Wang Chien-min (1965), *Zhongguo gongchandang shigao* [A draft history of the Chinese Communist Party], Taipei.

Wang Jianying (1983), *Zhongguo gongchandang zuzhishi ziliao huibian* [A collection of materials on the organisational history of the CCP], Beijing.

Wang Jiaxiang xuanji bianjizu (1985), *Huiyi Wang Jiaxiang* [Remembering Wang Jiaxiang], Beijing.

—— (1989), *Wang Jiaxiang xuanji* [Selected works of Wang Jiaxiang], Beijing.

Wang Jin (1992), *Mao Zedong da cidian* [A Mao Zedong dictionary], Nanning.

Wang, Ming (1979), *Mao's Betrayal.* Moscow.

Wang Shengrong (1984), 'Guanyu sanshi niandai zai Shanghai gongzuo de pianduan huiyi' [Some memories of the work in Shanghai in the 1930s]. *Shanghai dangshi ziliao tongxun,* 6, 17–22.

Wang Xiuxin (1992), 'Zhonggong zhongyang zhengzhiju shieryue huiyi he sanyue huiyi' [The December and March conferences of the CCP's Politburo]. *Zhonggong dangshi ziliao,* 44, 194–211.

—— (1993), 'Zhonggong liujie liuzhong quanhui' [The Sixth Plenum of the CCP's Sixth Central Committee]. Zhonggong dangshi ziliao 46, 228–254.

Wang Yifan (1988), 'Dui 1941 nian 9 yue zhengzhiju kuodahuiyi de buyi' [An addendum to the enlarged Politburo meeting in September 1941]. *Dangshi yanjiu ziliao*, 4, 26–29.

Weigelin-Schwiedrzik, Susanne (1984), *Parteigeschichtsschreibung in der VR China*. Wiesbaden.

Wilson, Dick (1971), *The Long March 1935*. New York.

—— (1984), *Chou – The Story of Zhou Enlai*. London.

Womack, Brantly (1982), *The Foundations of Mao Zedong's Political Thought*. Honolulu.

Wu T'ien-wei (1974), *Mao Tse-tung and the Tsunyi-Conference*. Washington.

Wu Xiuquan (1982), 'Wu Xiuquan tongzhi huiyilu (2)' [The memoirs of comrade Wu Xiuquan]. *Zhonggong dangshi ziliao*, 2, 160–218.

Wylie, Raymond F. (1980), *The Emergence of Maoism*. Stanford.

Xiang Qing (1994), *Sulian yu Zhongguo geming* [The Soviet Union and the Chinese Revolution], Beijing.

Xi'an shibianshi lingdao xiaozu (1986), *Xi'an shibian jianshi* [A short history of the Xi'an Incident], Beijing.

Xie Yan (1995), *Zhang Qinqiu de yisheng* [The life of Zhang Qinqiu], Beijing.

Xu Zehao (1991), *Wang Jiaxiang yanjiu lunji* [A collection of studies of Wang Jiaxiang], Hefei.

Yan'an zhengfeng yundong bianxiezu (1982), *Yan'an zhengfeng yundong jishi* [A chronology of the Yan'an rectification movement], Beijing.

Yang, Benjamin (1986), 'The Zunyi Conference as one step in Mao's rise to power'. *The China Quarterly*. no. 106, pp. 235–271.

—— (1990), *From Revolution to Politics: Chinese Communists on the Long March*. Boulder.

Yang Yunruo & Yang Kuisong (1988), *Gongchanguoji yu Zhongguo geming* [The Communist International and the Chinese revolution], Shanghai.

Yang Zhongmei (1989), *Zunyi huiyi yu Yan'an zhengfeng* [The Zunyi Conference and Yan'an rectification], Hong Kong.

Yao Weidou (1980), '"Mosike Zhongshan Daxue he Zhongguo geming" neirong jianjie' [An introduction to the contents of 'Sun Yat-sen University in Moscow and the Chinese Revolution'], *Dangshi yanjiu ziliao*, 2, 815ff.

Yi Shaolin (1994), 'Kai Feng' [Kai Feng], *Zhonggong dangshi renwuzhuan,* 52, Xi'an, 166–189.

Yuan Mengchao (1984), 'Yijiusansan nian Zhonggong Jiangsu shengwei de yixie qingkuang' [The situation in the CCP's Jiangsu provincial committee in 1933]. *Dangshi ziliao congkan,* 4, 3–7.

Zhang Xuexin (1994), *Ren Bishi zhuan* [A biography of Ren Bishi], Beijing.

Zhang Wentian xuanji bianjizu (1990), *Zhang Wentian wenji* (1) [Collected works of Zhang Wentian], Beijing.

—— (1993), *Zhang Wentian wenji (2)* [Collected works of Zhang Wentian], Beijing.

—— (1994), *Zhang Wentian wenji (3)* [Collected works of Zhang Wentian], Beijing.

Zheng Guangjin and Fang Shike (1987), *Zhongguo Hongjun chang-zheng ji* [The Long March of the Chinese Red Army], Zheng-zhou.

Zhengzhi xueyuan zhonggong dangshi jiaoyanshi (1985), *Zhongguo gong-chandang liushinian dashi jianjie* [A short introduction to major events in sixty years of CCP history], Beijing.

Zhonggong dangshi renwu yanjiuhui: *Zhonggong dangshi renwuzhuan* [Biographies of personalities in the history of the Chinese Communist Party], Xi'an.

Zhonggong zhongyang dangshi ziliao zhengji weiyuanhui (1985), *Zunyi huiyi wenxian* [Documents of the Zunyi Conference], Beijing.

Zhonggong zhongyang wenxian yanjiushi (1993), *Ren Bishi nianpu* [A chronicle of Ren Bishi], Beijing.

Zhongyang dang'anguan, *Zhonggong zhongyang wenjian xuanji* [Selected documents of the CCP's Central Committee], Beijing.

Zhou Guoquan (1990), *Wang Ming pingzhuan* [A critical biography of Wang Ming], Hefei.

Zunyi huiyi jinianguan (1990), *Zhang Wentian yu Zunyi huiyi* [Zhang Wentian and the Zunyi Conference], Beijing.

Index

The Nordic Institute of Asian Studies (NIAS) is funded by
the governments of Denmark, Finland, Iceland, Norway
and Sweden via the Nordic Council of Ministers, and
works to encourage and support Asian studies in the
Nordic countries. In so doing, NIAS has published well in
excess of one hundred books in the last three decades.

Nordic Council of Ministers

Printed by Printforce, United Kingdom